ACCOUNTABILITY

ACCOUNTABILITY

Freedom and Responsibility Without Control

Rob Lebow & Randy Spitzer

BK

BERRETT-KOEHLER PUBLISHERS, INC.
San Francisco

Berrett-Koehler Publishers, Inc.
235 Montgomery, Suite 650, San Francisco, CA 94104-2916
Tel: (415) 288-0260   Fax: (415) 362-2512   www.bkconnection.com

ORDERING INFORMATION

Quantity sales. Special discounts are available on quantity purchases by corporations, associations, and others. For details, contact the "Special Sales Department" at the Berrett-Koehler address above.

Individual sales. Berrett-Koehler publications are available through most bookstores. They can also be ordered direct from Berrett-Koehler:
Tel: (800) 929-2929; Fax: (802) 864-7626; www.bkconnection.com

Orders for college textbook/course adoption use. Please contact Berrett-Koehler: Tel: (800) 929-2929; Fax: (802) 864-7626.

Orders by U.S. trade bookstores and wholesalers. Please contact Publishers Group West, 1700 Fourth Street, Berkeley, CA 94710. Tel: (510) 528-1444; Fax (510) 528-3444.

Production Management: Michael Bass & Associates

Berrett-Koehler and the BK logo are registered trademarks of Berrett-Koehler Publishers, Inc.

Printed in the United States of America

Berrett-Koehler books are printed on long-lasting acid-free paper. When it is available, we choose paper that has been manufactured by environmentally responsible processes. These may include using trees grown in sustainable forests, incorporating recycled paper, minimizing chlorine in bleaching, or recycling the energy produced at the paper mill.

Library of Congress Cataloging-in-Publication Data

Lebow, Rob.
    Accountability : freedom and responsibility without control / by Rob
    Lebow and Randy Spitzer.
      p. cm.
    Includes bibliographical references and index.
    ISBN 1-57675-183-X
    1. Leadership. 2. Executive ability. 3. Organizational effectiveness.
  I. Spitzer, Randy, 1952– II. Title.
HD57.7 .L4385 2002
658.4´092—dc21   2002021582

First Edition
  05   04   03   02   10 9 8 7 6 5 4 3

Love is true freedom—to my two ladies,
Sharon and Lauren.
—R.L.

■ ■ ■

For my daughter Heather and my son Christof.
—R.S.

C O N T E N T S

Contents

P R O L O G U E

A NEW JOURNEY BEGINS

Accountability has become one of the most talked-about subjects of our time and perhaps the most perplexing of all people-related themes.

This story begins in Denver, Colorado, during the winter holiday season. Pete Williams, like thousands of other travelers in the Rocky Mountain states, has been stranded by an especially heavy snowstorm that has frozen the heartland of America.

Now, let's start our journey as Stan Kiplinger, a retired business executive, meets Pete Williams, the hard-charging CEO of an internationally recognized electronics manufacturer who has just transitioned his organization into the fiber optics business.

The Amtrak train was the only alternative to waiting out this snowstorm, and Pete Williams was not the kind of person who liked to wait. He boarded the 9:00 a.m. to Los Angeles with stops in Martinez and Bakersfield, California, and moved quickly past other passengers to compartment 417-C, sliding open the door.

It would take nearly two days to get to L.A. by train. Even though it would take much longer than flying, booking a seat on the train was a better alternative to sitting in a Denver hotel room hoping for a flight when the weather cleared. And, like most of the CEOs of his time, Pete was a take-charge executive who viewed time and money as inseparable commodities. Traveling by train would also give him time to think through what he was facing in Los Angeles and back at corporate headquarters. Just before boarding, Pete had momentarily looked at the name of the train, *The California Zephyr*. He knew what it meant—a gentle western wind.

As Pete opened the compartment door, he saw an older man who looked like a retired businessman. He noticed the man's casual clothing, accented by a gold Rolex watch on his left wrist that suggested this fellow must have made some money in his time.

Placing his bag above his seat, Pete turned and made eye contact with his overnight travel mate. "Hi, I'm Pete Williams. With the airport closed and my flight canceled, it looks like we'll be making this trip together."

The older man reached up and shook Pete's hand and said smiling, "My name's Stan Kiplinger, but everyone calls me Kip. I've been watching this storm dump snow since I boarded the train in Chicago. It'll be good to get to Los Angeles and feel warm sun again." The older man paused and then asked, "Are you going home for the holidays, or is this a business trip?"

"It's a business trip, I'm afraid," replied Pete with a frown. "I need to get to L.A. for a meeting with our business partners, but this blasted snowstorm trapped me in Denver. It couldn't have happened at a worse time." Pete realized he was expressing a lot of emotion to a perfect stranger, so he softened his tone. "But I guess that's life."

"It would seem so," said Kip empathetically. "If it's not too personal, what business are you in?"

"It's not too personal at all," said Pete, relaxing a bit. "I imagine we'll know a lot about each other before this trip's over. For the past forty-two years, my company was in the electronic parts business. Our business has been slowly dying because of all the changes in the industry. So to stay competitive I forced some drastic changes."

The younger man, reflecting on his experience, said, "I guess it's been about eighteen months now. My board of directors agreed to my radical idea of changing our business focus, but frankly, that's when all of my problems began.

"Maybe I pushed too hard. I remember having one heck of a time talking my senior staff into reinventing ourselves. Talk about challenges: I felt like a presidential candidate on the stump, shaking hands and kissing babies all the way!"

The older man nodded his head and laughed in support. "I bet it wasn't a cakewalk to get all your people to take the risk, huh?"

"No, it wasn't!" the younger man admitted. "I wanted to place our company squarely in the competitive arena of the fiber optics business. Kip, my people are good, and our reputation is solid, but many of our best customers were moving from the old brick-and-mortar parts business into the optics industry. We had to follow their move or look forward to closing our doors." Kip could see the seriousness on Pete's face.

"I believed then and I still do," Pete continued with conviction, "that our decision was a good one. But now I'm not sure if we can pull it off. It's almost like everyone is dead at the switch. I can't get the staff or my management team excited about the challenges facing us. It's as though they expect me to do all the thinking for them!"

"Oh?" said Kip.

Pete began unloading his troubles and fears on this seemingly sympathetic stranger. "Recently, we began manufacturing system components and optical fabrication supplies for a large multinational Japanese telecommunications provider. It was a big multimillion-dollar contract that made all the local papers. You know, the kind that a company can be built on."

Pete leaned forward and quickened his pace. "So, when we signed the contract, I thought that it was the best day of my life—outside of marrying my wife and later holding my infant daughter in my arms."

Pete paused and lowered his eyes before going on. "Our partnership is kind of shaky right now, so I'm personally going to L.A. to try and shore up the relationship. I frankly don't know if I'm going to be looking for a new job myself when this is all over. Maybe I took too much risk and asked the company to bite off more than it could chew."

Pete was still not looking at Kip but had his eyes on the floor. "I'm the genius who pushed everyone into this. Now I feel like a guy who's walking the plank. And, to add to my troubles, the board recently placed a new CFO—a real numbers guy—at the helm of our financial department. Frankly, I don't know if the guy is on my side or if he's a spy. I can't figure out the board's motives for hiring him, but I have this uneasy feeling." Then almost inaudibly Pete muttered, "I haven't slept well for weeks."

Kip sensed that he needed to cheer up his fellow traveler. "It sounds like you've got the weight of the world on your shoulders. I've been there and survived. I know you will, too."

Pete smiled a half-hearted smile, knowing that Kip was trying to cheer him up, and then said, "I wish it were only one or two problems, but there seem to be dozens. And the most frustrating thing is that I really can't put my finger on the key issue. I know I can handle the board, and I know that this new CFO won't be a problem if I can get the business moving.

"Kip, the business is there for the taking—but I can't do it alone. Believe me, I've thrown money, programs, staff, and outside experts at it, but the problems aren't going away. I've even tried restructuring our manufacturing divisions. I did that before the new CFO came on board and before we entered the optics market. It was tough sledding, restructuring the plants and shuffling around our leadership. I thought I'd really cleaned up our problems, but that's not how it's turned out.

"About a year ago I did the unthinkable—I took the risk of consulting with our partners on our quality issues. Among our partners is one of the best-run Japanese companies in America, and when I approached them on helping us sort out our quality problems, they were great about it." Pete shook his head. "I thought I'd lose some of my top guys over this. Kip, you wouldn't believe some of my peoples' egos! Admitting to outsiders that we may not know everything was too much for some of my key managers. Instead of seeing our partners as partners—true partners—my people saw these folks as the enemy.

"But even with all this spent energy and the feather ruffling, the end results are the same: we still can't get people to be accountable for their performance, even though our systems and procedures have improved. And this problem is felt at every level. It isn't just in the hourly ranks. It's everywhere!

"People seem to lack the will," continued Pete, "to take personal responsibility for the goals we set and the deadlines we establish. They sit in the conference rooms with my top managers and me. They agree to the goals and the timetables in the meeting, but once outside and back to their own areas, they complain about how unfair we are.

"I believe in giving everyone a chance to speak—but most won't." Hesitating, Pete decided to share one last tidbit of information. "We've threatened folks with their livelihoods, not something I liked doing, but not even that worked. We've spent millions of dollars on incentive programs to no avail. Frankly, I'm at my wit's end."

Kip could see that Pete was feeling the pressure. It showed on his face and in his body language.

Pete didn't know why he was unloading on this stranger, but this older man seemed to listen with the ear of an experienced problem solver. "Kip, I apologize if I'm dumping a load of woes on you, but for some reason, you seem to want to hear about it—I mean, truly hear about it." Smiling broadly, he added, "I hope you don't call the conductor and have me thrown off the train!"

Kip appreciated Pete's sense of humor yet understood the weight of his remarks. He wanted Pete to know that he was eager to listen. "Pete, I do want to hear about it. From my experience you're not alone. Your problems, it seems to me, are common. Most of what you're relating has happened to me." He turned to Pete with a mock smile and crooked his head in a Clintonian posture. "I feel your pain!" The tension broke as both men laughed at the reference.

"But seriously, Pete, in board meetings I attend and in private conversations with workers and supervisors, everyone at every level shares similar complaints. People seem to be into the blame game. No one wants to listen any more.

Managers place too much pressure on the staff, and the staff feels powerless to do anything about it. People resent the pressure. They resent being asked to perform without being listened to."

Kip sensed that he had Pete's attention now and his confidence. "We live in a time when e-mail has become a contact sport. We shout at each other demanding our rights, thinking if we shout loud enough that we'll be heard. And we all seem to feel disconnected from our own organizations, even the best spirited of us.

"Many companies falsely think they're solving their people issues by letting people work at home so that they won't have to interact with each other on a daily basis. But these organizations are only putting their heads in the sand. It's like the doctor who shoots up an athlete's knee with novocaine and sends him back into the game without considering the long-term effects." Pete laughed, really understanding what Kip was saying.

"Workers complain about their bosses not having the guts to step up to the tough issues. Supervisors tell me they feel like they're standing in the middle of a minefield with no confidence in their next step. And the top executive's predicament is the saddest of all; they have no one to talk to. Talk about feeling isolated!" Pete identified completely.

"In fact, most of the senior executives with whom I've spoken over the years feel like they're victimized by their own organizations. They feel overwhelmed by the weight of responsibility that goes with the top job. . . ."

"Tell me about it!" interjected Pete.

". . . And they feel frustrated that others in the organization don't seem to share their passion for the business or support the goals that'll make the company successful.

"Pete, you said it earlier. They, like you, feel they're walking a plank with alligators waiting open-mouthed in the water below. It seems everyone at every level is struggling to identify the problem. Some think it's a lack of commitment by employees to their jobs or a lack of involvement. Others say it is people not wanting or willing to take responsibility. Some are convinced it has to do with the generation gap. Still others see it as an organizational structure problem or system weakness. But to me, it comes down to one issue."

Pete leaned toward Kip and broke in. "OK, if it's that simple, what's the issue? What's the one thing that I'm facing?"

Kip responded immediately, picking up his pace. "Pete, you mentioned it when you said that you couldn't get people to be *accountable* for their performance." Kip held up one finger on his right hand and said, punctuating his comment, "Accountability is the issue! If you can't find a way to get people to be accountable, you're going to find it hard to make anything work, let alone your business.

Accountability is the issue! If you can't find a way to get people to be accountable, you're going to find it hard to make anything else work, let alone your business.

"But, getting people to be accountable requires that you stop trying to *impose* accountability on them. If you try to force them to be responsible, they'll only resent your demands, and I guarantee they'll fight back, sometimes in ways you can see, but most often in ways you can't."

"You're right about that," nodded Pete.

"Pete, here is what it comes down to. When you force people to do anything, the human tendency to resist kicks in. I resent someone forcing me to do something, and I'd bet you do, too. So why expect this approach to work on anyone else? Forcing someone to do something is just another way of controlling them. The key is to find a way to lead people without ruling them!

The key is to find a way to lead people without ruling them!

"I've come to understand that trying to control people just doesn't work. But getting this concept through my thick Scottish skull hasn't been easy. It's taken years," smiled Kip.

"I've learned that getting people to be accountable requires adopting a totally new philosophy about people: people want to be great; in fact, they *need* to be great!

"Pete, we all want to work with people who are accountable. Even a frontline worker expects those around her or him to be accountable. But getting everyone to be accountable isn't easy. I've come to accept an approach about this whole subject that in my younger days I'd have rejected out of hand. I would have called it crazy! I now know that when people are free to own their jobs and to take control of their results, responsibility is placed in the right hands. It comes down to something really simple: are we going to control people, or are they going to be free to make choices?

"I was the boss for many years. In the old days I thought I was a darn fine boss. Now, I know I wasn't because I was trying to force results by using controls." Kip paused, and Pete could see that Kip was serious.

The silence was broken by a knock at the compartment door. The conductor slid the door partially open and said, "Excuse me, gentlemen, but we'll be departing in just a moment. May I see your tickets?"

A few moments later, the train inched forward. The weight of the train caused the wheels of the three great engines to churn ever so slowly. Most of the passengers settled in their compartments as the train's pace quickened and the vista changed to a more rural, snow-covered landscape.

Pete Williams, a CEO with lots of troubles on his mind, and Stan Kiplinger, a man willing to listen and to share his insights, began their journey together. And maybe, just maybe, Pete's time with Kip would forever change his thinking about accountability.

PART ONE

THE
CONTROL
versus
FREEDOM
DILEMMA

1

I'm Pedaling as Fast as I Can, But It's Not Fast Enough!

The *California Zephyr* was at full speed when Pete verbalized the thoughts he was having about what Kip had just said. "I agree accountability is a big issue, but I don't think you can get people to be accountable without sensible controls in place.

"Kip, if you're suggesting in any way that I should ease up on my managers and staff, you're crazy. And I'm not saying this to be tough. I'm saying it to be realistic. I have no experience that suggests that giving up control will get me or my company to the finish line." Pete realized that he might be coming on a little too strong, but he needed to let Kip know that he wasn't from the "let's all hold hands" school of leadership.

"Pete, at one point in my career I'd have agreed with you," said Kip. "In fact, it literally took a heart attack to change my mind on the whole subject. Before that life-changing event, I prided myself on being a tough, but fair, boss. I thought leadership meant that you played the game like the legendary Lone Ranger—fighting the bad guys single-handedly. I was just fifty-three years old and the CEO of National Stores. Perhaps you've heard of them?"

Pete answered. "Of course I've heard of National Stores. We have one in the mall near our house."

Kip continued. "Like the Lone Ranger, I was playing the only role I knew how to play—the guy with *all* the silver bullets! I was the visionary leader with the white ten-gallon hat, full of my own self-importance. I was the main man.

"Pete," Kip added with a smirk, "I was full of it! I was on top of the heap yet shaking in my boots for fear that the bubble would burst at any moment. I was secretly miserable and afraid to admit my fears, even to my wife until my heart attack."

"What's this about a heart attack?" asked Pete with concern.

"Well, I'd been CEO of National Stores for about three years after a thirty-year climb to the top. I was working between eighty and one hundred hours per week and was on the road constantly. My wife and family had become strangers to me. I was missing the best years of my life and didn't even know it. When I wasn't visiting one of our stores trying to put out a fire, I was negotiating with our bankers to restructure our debt.

"Pete, I had so many balls in the air, I couldn't see the sky let alone smell the roses. I was out of touch and in a tailspin."

"It sounds like more of a death spiral to me," commiserated Pete with a laugh. He realized now that he was not alone and that Kip had survived the ordeal—maybe he would, too.

Kip didn't miss a beat. "Like you, I was under a great deal of pressure from our board to improve our company's slumping performance." Kip recognized that what he was saying was having an impact on the younger man.

"Your story sounds all too familiar," said Pete uncomfortably.

"Hopefully, *this* part of my story you'll never experience." Taking a deeper breath, Kip paused. This was hard for him to talk about. "It was on a Monday morning, twenty-one years ago in early November. I was getting out of bed when I felt chest pains. It felt like an NFL linebacker was sitting on me—I was suffocating. I'd just had my company physical, and the doctor had asked me some pointed questions that I'd blown off.

"Looking back, I can see he was asking me if I needed help, but I didn't hear him—I wasn't listening. My test results were marginal. That's another way of saying, 'Hello, you're on thin ice.' The numbers indicated that I was a middle-aged guy whose body was showing the effects of a lot of stress. But I thought I was Superman."

Pete knew exactly what Kip was talking about. "Yeah, my wife is always on my case about taking some time for me. I used to love to run, but since my knee surgery, it's been hard to find the time to work out."

Kip nodded and went on. "Well, that morning my wife, who normally would have already been on her way to work, was still home. She must have sensed something. I insisted that it was just indigestion, but she called 911 anyway— thank goodness! I don't know what would have happened if I'd been in some lonely hotel room or the only one at home that morning.

"Lucky for me, the attack was a mild one. But before I was released from the hospital, my doctor was blunt. No, he was brutal. He said, 'Either change your lifestyle or plan on an early grave.' *That* got my attention!"

"I imagine it would," said Pete with a grimace. "I must admit that I'm beginning to be concerned with my pace and whether I can keep it up forever. Sometimes I'm not sure I can pedal any faster."

Kip nodded in understanding and went on. "The business depended on me, or at least I thought so at the time. And frankly, I didn't see anyone on my staff who was ready to take on my responsibilities, let alone the pressures. More important, I wasn't ready to let go because I loved being in charge. Yet I knew if I didn't give my staff the freedom to help me carry the load, the job would kill me. I knew this, but I had no alternative. At least, that's what I thought at the time.

"Pete, something had to give, and it was me. My heart attack had forced me into a dilemma: Either hold onto control and face the consequences to my health, or give my staff the reins."

"So what did you do?" asked Pete.

"Well, first, I went through the denial phase," explained Kip. "Then I got angry, like it was the darn doctor's fault. But

I eventually realized that if I had problems, it was me who would have to change. So here's what I did. About a week after I got out of the hospital, I called my executive team together at my home and explained my situation.

"I told my staff things needed to change, and, more important, I needed to change. I said that the biggest changes needed to come from me, not from them. Frankly, Pete, at that point, I had nothing to lose; I was already losing my business, I was losing my health, and, worst of all, I was losing my family. I admitted that I didn't know if I could give up control. I admitted my vulnerabilities to the men and women who had depended on me.

"Every one of them reacted in a way I hadn't expected. They already knew! I mean, they knew I was in a death spiral. The only surprise to them was that I had lasted as long as I had."

For some reason, Pete thought this was funny and laughed. "Kip, I couldn't help but laugh. If what you are telling me wasn't so serious, it would be funny."

Kip nodded and smiled. "You're absolutely right. Looking back on the whole mess that I had created makes me want to laugh *and* cry. But at the time, I was taking myself pretty seriously.

"I asked my people why they'd never spoken to me about it. And do you know what they said? They were afraid of me. They were afraid of my anger and afraid of being fired.

"They knew what needed to be done at work and knew how to address many of the recurring problems, but they were afraid to share them with me. At that moment I realized that I was both the problem and the solution.

"The problem was my controlling behavior, and the solution was to let go of control. But letting go of control was totally alien to me. My challenge was to trust the people around me, something that was not natural for me.

The problem was my controlling behavior,
and the solution was to let go of control.

"Of course, that's what should've happened years earlier. But I had learned from my boss, and he had learned from his. The only role models I had were control freaks. And I was the best control freak you ever saw."

"Funny you say that," said Pete. "That phrase keeps coming up all around my company. Our people take pride in being control freaks. I think it's kind of crazy, but it seems to be the rule."

Kip nodded in understanding. "Pete, we would literally have gone out of business, not because we didn't have the talent or the creative ideas. No, we'd have gone out of business because of my stubbornness."

These last words cut deep into Pete's heart. He resonated with these words and didn't like where they led.

The sun shone high overhead and reflected off the carpet of snow into the train compartment. Compartment 417-C had become a confessional as two strangers shared their innermost secrets, their vulnerabilities, and their fears. The wheels of the train clacked along the tracks. The steady rhythm supported the conversation by filling in the pauses.

2

The Courage to Make the Change

Kip continued relating his story because he felt he had to. "My brother, who was an alcoholic, hit rock bottom in the late seventies," he said in a matter-of-fact voice. "I remember the call from my older sister that one cold fall night. She said he'd wrapped his car around a tree. That was his wake-up call. He joined AA shortly after.

"Alcoholics Anonymous was the best thing that ever happened to him and his family. The lessons my brother learned and that I learned after my heart attack were similar. First, admit you have a problem, then accept the fact that it's within your power to make the changes you need to make.

"Sure, you'll need help. No one can do it all by himself. But *you* must take the first step." Kip was trying to be direct but respectful with his fellow CEO.

"When I admitted to my staff that I had a problem, I gave myself choices, and that was a great gift. Believe me, Pete, you have lots of alternatives, and I don't mean fancy programs or silver bullets."

Pete was intrigued. In fact, he was moved. "I can pretty much guess the changes you made in your personal life, but what alternatives did you explore at work?" he asked.

"I first started exploring alternatives with the people who were most affected by my behavior," Kip replied pointedly. "Our first attempts at change were sincere but flawed. They were flawed because I was still looking for a program. I thought if I could find the right program, our problems would disappear.

"We tried total quality management (TQM). Remember in the mid-eighties it was the rage, and it made sense at the time. And we enrolled our people in personal improvement courses; I even took on a personal coach. I brought in consultants to help us design a new incentive program, we installed a customer service initiative, and we outsourced our help desk facilities. We tried every program we thought was reasonable. Still, we saw no real sustainable improvement to our bottom line. And our people didn't seem to be any more accountable."

Kip could see that Pete was engrossed in what he was saying. The last thing he wanted to do was to bore anyone with his ideas.

Pete looked at Kip and asked, "OK, so what did you finally do?"

"One afternoon as I was driving home after another frustrating day, it came to me. I was so excited about the idea that I stopped my car on the side of the road and called the one senior staff member who'd always tell me when I was off base—my retail operations vice president, Jennifer Bailey. This was before cell phones. I can recall the experience to this day. I had to speak—no, I had to shout to be heard on the pay phone by the side of the highway.

"Imagine the scene: I'm telling her about my great epiphany as I'm shouting into this phone while holding my hand over my left ear as the trucks whizzed by." Kip chuckled as he related the story.

"What did she say?" asked Pete.

"I thought she'd laugh, but she didn't. Jennifer Bailey, the one person I knew who would tell me flat-out if I was all wet, said, 'What took you so long to figure it out?' Pete, that was the beginning of my journey.

"It seemed simple standing out on that highway and talking to Jennifer, but what happened over the next several years wasn't easy. Frankly, it turned out to be the hardest three years in my business career. But it saved me, it saved our business, and it saved my relationship with everyone I cared about."

Pete sensed that this man was about to tell him something important. "What was your epiphany?" he asked with anticipation.

"Pete, what I told Jennifer was simple. 'People work better when they're free to do it their way.' *That* was my epiphany.

"Did I want my staff to live in fear that they would say or do something wrong? Or did I want them to be free to do their job as they saw fit, to the best of their abilities?

> *Did I want my staff to live in fear that they would say or do something wrong? Or did I want them to be free to do their job as they saw fit, to the best of their abilities?*

"The epiphany was an either/or choice. Choosing freedom would strip all of our control-based assumptions and challenge our capacity to trust our people. Choosing freedom would mean that every staff member at every level would be fully accountable for his or her ideas, actions, behaviors, and performance, without anyone looking over his or her shoulder. No more alibis, passing the buck, or playing the blame game, and no second-guessing on performance reviews. To me, it meant that I would no longer accept the 'helpless victim' role from my staff. And it meant for the first time we'd enjoy an adult-to-adult relationship."

Pete began thinking about the consequences of Kip's ideas on his business. He knew that Kip was personally challenging him to make a fundamental choice between *control* and *freedom*. That's why Kip was telling him this story. Would he continue to choose a control-based approach to business, or would he abandon the idea of controlling others in favor of freedom? These were uncharted waters for Pete.

Pete's began playing out different scenarios in his mind. Could he trust his people to do their jobs? Pete realized that even thinking like this was dangerous.

Shaking his head, Pete muttered to himself, "No, it isn't possible." Given his present circumstances, this was the wrong time to even consider something like this. It would be nuts, and he'd be signing his own career's death warrant.

Kip knew that abandoning control was pretty radical. He had experienced this reaction over the past years with many business leaders. He himself would have reacted the same way if some stranger had offered the freedom philosophy as a solution early in his career.

"Pete, remember what Jennifer said: 'What took you so long?' She had already figured out that all the programs we were trying wouldn't solve our fundamental problem—getting people to own their jobs and to be accountable. She knew that personal coaching, measurement tools, and incentives might be helpful but that the fundamental issue still remained untouched. I guess she was a lot smarter than I was. It took me over a year after my heart attack to recognize that believing in people was the missing piece of the puzzle.

"Since I retired from National Stores, I've been sharing this philosophy—that you must abandon the idea of controlling people—with business leaders who have hit brick walls. I guess you could call it my mission in life." Kip smiled and continued.

"They've hit this wall after decades of trying control-based programs, systems, and processes that seem always to fall short of the promised benefits. The lesson I learned from Jennifer and others was that the more you try to control people, the less responsible and accountable they become.

The more you try to control people, the less responsible and accountable they become.

"The funny thing is that business leaders will try just about every crazy idea, gimmick, or program under the sun before they're willing to consider a freedom-based approach of trusting people and treating them like adults!

"Jennifer recognized a fundamental truth about human nature that I didn't—that people want to be great. And not only do they *want* to be great, but also they *need* to be great, and they need their freedom to achieve great things.

"Before my eyes were opened that afternoon, National Stores focused on facilities management, store locations, marketing and merchandising, distribution systems, inventory control, centralized purchasing, and sales training. We forgot the simplest of lessons that everyone wants to be free to choose to do it *their* way. And, if you let them do it their way, the possibilities are darn near infinite."

Intrigued but still skeptical, Pete wanted to know more. "Kip, I appreciate everything you're saying, but you said earlier that the one issue facing me was accountability, that everything came down to this one issue. So, exactly how does freedom produce accountability?"

Kip smiled and welcomed the direct question. "Pete, you've asked the right question." The older man sat back in a reflective posture and raised his eyes to the ceiling of compartment 417-C. Before he spoke again, he refocused his eyes on Pete. "That's the piece of the puzzle I didn't see at first. But Jennifer—good ol' Jennifer—did. Here's what it boils down to: You cannot control people and ever expect them to be accountable. Or, put in the reverse, to create personal accountability at every level, you need to establish a freedom-based workplace at every level."

"You've got to be kidding," said Pete with astonishment. "How in heaven's name do I do that?"

At Pete's last declaration, Kip put his briefcase on his lap and searched through it while he talked. "Pete, here's the easiest way I can explain how you do it.

"When I returned to the National Stores offices that next morning, I cleared my calendar and asked Jennifer and another senior team member, my merchandising director, Brad Copler, to help me put together our transition plan."

You cannot control people and ever expect them to be accountable. Or, put in the reverse, to create personal accountability at every level, you need to establish a freedom-based workplace at every level.

Pete interrupted, "A transition plan?"

"OK, what I mean is that I realized that if we were going to abandon control-based thinking, we'd better know as much as we could about what old strategies we needed to abandon and what new strategies we were going to embrace. Ah, here it is," Kip exclaimed as he pulled a paper from his briefcase.

Without missing a beat, he continued. "I called it our transition plan. Jennifer and Brad helped me focus on this new approach and thinking. Eventually, I hoped everyone would know what we were talking about, where this was taking us as a company, and what changes and new commitments we needed to make."

"I see," said Pete, with some admiration. "It makes sense."

Kip went on while he handed the paper he'd found to Pete. "That day, we crafted this 'T-chart' because it was the most straightforward way to explain where we were and where we were going or, put another way, what we were abandoning and what we were embracing."

Pete looked at the chart while Kip spoke. "We organized the left side by the systems or processes that we presently had in place, the program and tools that controlled us. We ultimately abandoned *everything* on the left side of the chart, all three strategies. Not right away, mind you, but over a course of three to four years." Kip first detailed the left side of the T-chart—the control-based approach.

"We had worked on our structures for years. So, we identified the very first control-based element—'*Impose Authority*.' Our hierarchy was defined by our organizational chart. Next, we looked at how we approached supervision. We also identified a more subtle form of imposed authority that might surprise you. It was our quota systems.

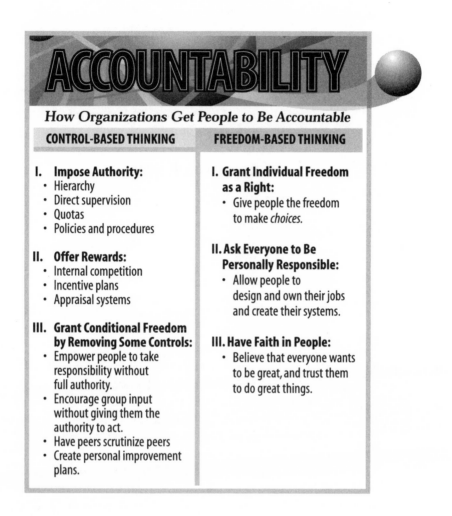

ACCOUNTABILITY

How Organizations Get People to Be Accountable

CONTROL-BASED THINKING	FREEDOM-BASED THINKING
I. Impose Authority: • Hierarchy • Direct supervision • Quotas • Policies and procedures	**I. Grant Individual Freedom as a Right:** • Give people the freedom to make *choices*.
II. Offer Rewards: • Internal competition • Incentive plans • Appraisal systems	**II. Ask Everyone to Be Personally Responsible:** • Allow people to design and own their jobs and create their systems.
III. Grant Conditional Freedom by Removing Some Controls: • Empower people to take responsibility without full authority. • Encourage group input without giving them the authority to act. • Have peers scrutinize peers • Create personal improvement plans.	**III. Have Faith in People:** • Believe that everyone wants to be great, and trust them to do great things.

"We concluded that quotas were a more subtle form of imposed authority, and, oh boy, were they prevalent at National Stores! Brad, Jennifer, and I really challenged each other on this one. In the end, they convinced me that quotas had to go if we were to stop imposing authority on our people.

"The fourth element under 'Impose Authority' were all the 'Policies and Procedures,' and I didn't need much convincing on this one." Kip smiled as he completed his explanation of the first category.

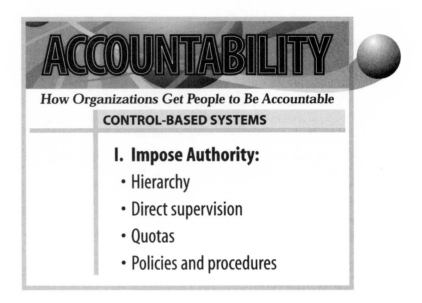

ACCOUNTABILITY

How Organizations Get People to Be Accountable

CONTROL-BASED SYSTEMS

I. Impose Authority:
- Hierarchy
- Direct supervision
- Quotas
- Policies and procedures

As Kip wrote out the first series of elements on a blank piece of paper, Pete quietly read them over and said nothing. Kip had ticked off the elements like he was reading a list of things you'd take on a camping trip, but Pete knew that each element had its own power base and momentum, along with a survival instinct deadlier than a cornered rattlesnake.

Kip's momentum, like the train's, was now unstoppable. Pete stared intently at the T-chart. He could not imagine throwing out all of the processes and systems that he and his fellow executives had labored so intensively to set in place. It seemed unfathomable that the older man was actually proposing that he abandon what was universally accepted—at least in the United States and most Western business environments—as the sound way to run a business enterprise.

Was he hearing Kip correctly? Could such a concept work? He wasn't sure, but he knew he had to hear more.

3

Which Would You Rather Work In— A Freedom-Based or a Control-Based Work Environment?

Pete broke in. "Let me see if I've got this." His tone had an air of disbelief. "You're telling me that you were prepared to get rid of your hierarchy, supervision, quotas, policies, and procedures? How did you keep your job?" Pete's incredulity was written all over his face.

Looking at Pete, Kip couldn't help but give out a belly laugh for the first time that day. "I not only kept my job, but I became one popular guy," Kip beamed with pride. "I mean, folks actually cheered when they heard about us abandoning control!"

"What about the supervisors? Did they cheer, too?" asked Pete, with apparent skepticism.

"No, not exactly," Kip said with candor and a smirk. "Some did, of course, but most didn't. Some were scared to death, while others were paralyzed by thoughts of the staff taking over the place. You know, they had visions of the inmates running the prison." Kip smiled, but it was evident that Pete wasn't amused as he folded his arms and moved slightly away from Kip.

As Kip continued, you could see that he was having fun sticking it to his younger and now noticeably stiffer colleague with all this revolutionary talk. "Supervisors at every level kept asking me how their jobs would get done. My phone rang off the hook in the early days, but I gave the supervisors the straight answer—I never faltered. I told them straight out, 'It's no longer your job. It's theirs!'"

Trying to alleviate Pete's obvious discomfort, Kip quickly added, "Please understand, Pete, we didn't run out to the stores and institute all these changes that same week—we might have been crazy, but we weren't stupid! No, we took our time. We planned for this change over several years, but that part of the story will come later, so let me go on." Pete sat back, a little more confident that he wasn't sharing a train compartment with a madman. He unfolded his arms but still maintained his distance, just in case.

"It took us all morning to sort through the first category because it was hard for me to let go of these controls. As we began to talk among ourselves during lunch, Brad came up with the notion that offering rewards was a form of control that was strangling us. We began to recognize that he was right. So the second category we called 'Offering Rewards.' Brad identified two of the elements in this category; Jennifer came up with the third."

Who invented the modern corporation? Men like John D. Rockefeller of Standard Oil, and Alfred Sloan of General Motors. In the postwar era of economic expansion, you had Robert McNamara at Ford and Harold Geneen at ITT, Reginald Jones at General Electric. It was the heyday of multiplex managerial strata, with chief executives assisted by staffs of planners and auditors and operations strategists. Rigid structures were necessary to conserve and manage the scarcest resource of all, the most valuable resource of all—information. Now, what happens if information becomes as free and copiously available as the air we breathe or the water we drink? All that becomes unnecessary. All that gives way.

—Gregson Manning, in *The Prometheus Deception* by Robert Ludlum
(New York: St. Martin's, 2000)

By now Pete was leaning forward again and looking more relaxed. He realized that Kip was unfolding for him what would amount to revolutionary changes. He was an experienced manager and had grown up in a corporate environment that thrived on controls as its staple diet. He understood instinctively that each control element comprised part of an entrenched bureaucracy. And he knew that these controls had taken on lives of their own and wouldn't just roll over and go away without a fight.

"Brad felt that internal competition and incentive plans were subtle forms of control," continued Kip. "We talked about this for some time. Internal competition, something many of us were raised on, became the number one element in this second category."

Pete looked puzzled, then spoke. "I'm a little confused. Isn't it a good thing to have internal competition?"

Kip nodded knowingly. "I thought so, too, Pete, but as Brad began to relate all the downside activities, such as cheating, withholding information, sabotaging colleagues, backstabbing, entitlements, and bad-mouthing, it appeared to us that his comments needed to be heeded."

Kip waited for a response from Pete, but it never came. Pete's only signal that he had heard Kip was a resigned nod, that Kip was right and that he, too, knew of these things in his career. And at that moment, Pete was reflecting on the brewing internal competition between himself and the new CFO at his optics company, something he wasn't looking forward to facing.

Kip brought Pete back to the present. "Jennifer thought the appraisal system should be in the second category, too. I didn't need much convincing, and neither did Brad. I thought back to a time when I was being appraised, and I didn't like it. Here's a short story to make my point.

"I was in my late twenties and flying high. That winter we got a new boss. He came in and started to review all of us. I was, at that time, leading the branch and second in the nation in sales. My numbers were great. The appraisal system was composed of a one to five ranking, with five being the top. Did I get all fives? Not on your life! My new boss gave me

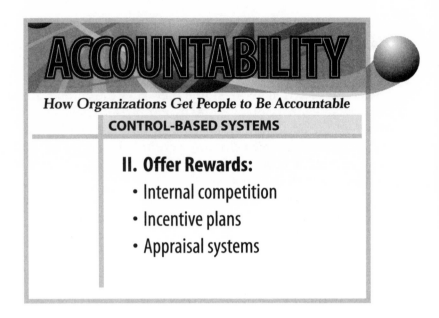

ACCOUNTABILITY

How Organizations Get People to Be Accountable

CONTROL-BASED SYSTEMS

II. Offer Rewards:

- Internal competition
- Incentive plans
- Appraisal systems

all fours! And why? Because, he said, if he gave me all fives, there wouldn't be any place for me to grow. I instantly hated him and left the branch at the first chance of a transfer. Do appraisals systems control people? I'll let you answer that," said Kip earnestly.

"OK, so the second category," summed Pete, "covers internal competition, incentive plans, and appraisal systems, and you're saying these need to go, too?" He had just a hint of resignation in his voice.

"Yes, I am," said Kip. "At National Stores we slam-dunked these three into the garbage can." The vision of Kip playing basketball was a little much for Pete, and he smiled.

"And, after we explained our reasoning to our staff, there weren't many who opposed this move. I know you have questions, but let me go on."

The older man next turned to the third category and the final four elements. Pete now leaned even closer to Kip and began reading upside down what Kip had written. Pete had learned to read upside down like many students do, and he

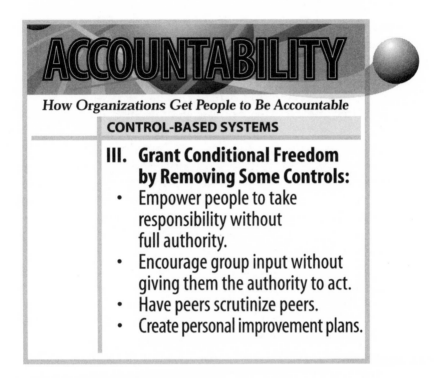

ACCOUNTABILITY

How Organizations Get People to Be Accountable

CONTROL-BASED SYSTEMS

III. Grant Conditional Freedom by Removing Some Controls:
- Empower people to take responsibility without full authority.
- Encourage group input without giving them the authority to act.
- Have peers scrutinize peers.
- Create personal improvement plans.

had refined the technique during his years of negotiating with unions.

Kip continued debriefing his fellow passenger. "I wanted to establish National Stores as a place where every staff member would take personal responsibility for his or her actions, decisions, and results.

"So, we abandoned the elements in this third category. Jennifer made the case for abandoning any attempts to delegate authority. She said we should either do it ourselves or let the other person or group do it. And if we let others take on responsibility, we shouldn't follow up on them. If we wanted people to be accountable, then we needed to treat them like adults.

"Pete, by the time we were discussing this third category, I wasn't sure I was going to have a business left. I was the one who had come up with the idea of abandoning controls the night before, but now that Pandora's box was open, it scared even me."

"That's the second time I've heard you use that phrase," said Pete.

"What's that?" said Kip.

"The one about treating people like adults. I always thought I *was* treating my people like adults, but after reading this list and hearing your explanation, I realize that I'm playing the parent role and not letting them behave as adults. I'm treating them like children."

Kip smiled and recognized that Pete was beginning to personalize these ideas. Kip wasn't sure how much of his argument Pete was buying, but at least Pete was trying the ideas on for size.

Pete continued. "But I don't understand how you eliminate following up on people and still ensure that they do what they're supposed to do."

Kip looked at Pete and for the first time seemed a little impatient with him. "Pete, we replaced follow-up with personal accountability. We made the person who took on the responsibility directly accountable, with no middle man or woman to see that the job got done."

"But what happened to all the supervisors?" asked Pete.

"Our supervisors still had plenty to do, but they weren't wiping noses anymore. The 'kids' had learned to tie their own shoes and go out to play," said Kip with a half smile and a wink, "and they loved it!"

It all began to sink in at some level for Pete, but he wasn't fully ready to accept what Kip was saying. "Are you trying to tell me, Kip, that none of the high-profile programs, systems, or processes you mentioned helped your company improve? We've implemented some of those same programs, and we've seen improvement. In fact, I'd argue that it's because we've added sensible controls that things have gotten better. Without these controls in place, I believe my people would be less accountable, not more."

"I understand your point," said Kip, "but what I'm saying is you don't need controls to get people to be accountable, and that's what I realized. And the experience I've had instituting this approach has been powerful beyond my imagination. I'd submit to you that people at every level within your operation are much more capable and willing to be accountable than you think, and that even sensible or subtle control programs are ultimately counterproductive. In fact, to see greater accountability, you've got to give up control totally and give people the freedom to be accountable. That's the paradox. But there is good news, too. Your people are *ready* for the change.

"Maybe we should now take a look at the right side of the chart so you'll see what we did."

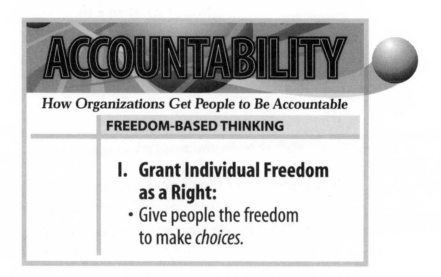

ACCOUNTABILITY

How Organizations Get People to Be Accountable

FREEDOM-BASED THINKING

I. Grant Individual Freedom as a Right:
- Give people the freedom to make *choices*.

Pete welcomed the suggestion and said, "Please, by all means."

Pete read the three new categories. He held his tongue until he couldn't any longer. "Kip, I just can't buy this approach and here's why. I have 10 to 20 percent of my people doing 80 percent of the work. That means there are a lot of people who would run wild under your approach. Sure, 10 to 20 percent of my people might do well under your system, but I have 80 to 90 percent of my people who would take advantage of us if we instituted anything like this. Heck, *with*

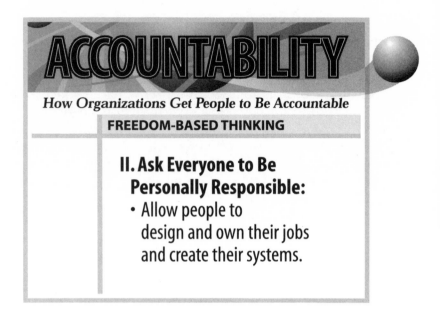

ACCOUNTABILITY

How Organizations Get People to Be Accountable

FREEDOM-BASED THINKING

II. Ask Everyone to Be Personally Responsible:
- Allow people to design and own their jobs and create their systems.

controls they aren't producing; now you want me to treat them like adults? How do you respond to that?"

I'd submit to you that people at every level within your operation are much more capable and willing to be accountable than you think, and that even sensible or subtle control programs are ultimately counterproductive.

Kip took this opportunity to poke some fun at Pete. "Pete, who's to blame for this situation? Was the hiring process at your company so poor that this happened, or did your control systems kill the potential of 80 percent of your people?" Even Pete had to laugh at Kip's comment, but Kip had made his point. The point was clear: Controls weren't the solution, but Pete still wasn't ready to recognize it.

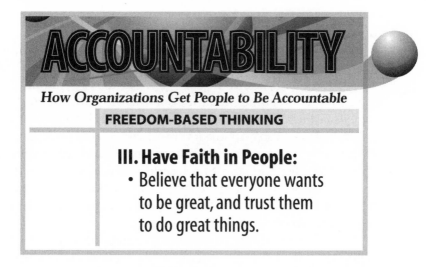

ACCOUNTABILITY

How Organizations Get People to Be Accountable

FREEDOM-BASED THINKING

III. Have Faith in People:
* Believe that everyone wants to be great, and trust them to do great things.

"We realized that our beliefs about people were holding us back," Kip explained further. "The solution was to give up control. The challenge was, could we ultimately trust people? Because if we couldn't, these new ideas would never work.

"I came to believe that we had never been in control and that we were literally killing our people's spirit. Control was an illusion, like looking out the window of this train and feeling as if you're going backward, when what's really happening is that a train next to you is pulling forward and tricking your senses into thinking you're moving backward."

Shaking his head, Pete broke in. "I'm sorry, but I'm just not comfortable with the idea of giving up control. Yes, I want to trust my people, but . . . ." His voice trailed off.

Kip smiled in understanding. "It was tough for me as a CEO to give up control. I was 'Mr. Control' himself! But I ultimately realized it was even tougher to control people who resented being controlled." He paused for a moment to let his message sink in. "Pete, before you became a CEO, how did you feel when your boss tried to control you?"

Pete immediately answered, "I hated it and it made me mad! I felt that he didn't trust me."

"I'd bet the people at every level of your operation feel the same way," said Kip.

Pete nodded in agreement. "That's a sobering thought I never before considered, but I've got a question for you. Don't you think management has a right and responsibility to maintain at least some measure of control? Without controls in place, I'm afraid my operation would sink into anarchy."

"Pete, please don't misunderstand me; it's not easy for people who have known nothing but control-based management systems to make the leap to a freedom-based work environment. I include in this statement both labor and management. Both have a lot of learning to do. But once they've tasted freedom, there's no going back."

"That *sounds* great," said Pete in mock agreement, "but can you give me a real-life example of a well-known company that's successfully made the transformation from a control-based management system to a freedom-based work environment and still stayed in business?"

"Sure!" said Kip. "Harley-Davidson is a wonderful example. In 1981 when the management of Harley-Davidson bought the company back from AMF, they were mired in controls and red ink. And they'd be the first to admit that, at the time, the bikes they were producing were, in their own words, 'junk'!

"The management team at Harley did one thing really right, but it wasn't until they tried a lot of control-based programs that didn't work that a miracle happened. They visited a Honda plant in Pennsylvania and what they saw blew their minds. Here was a plant of more than seven hundred people that had less than ten managers and only a couple of people who compiled the quality numbers on the bikes—and their bikes were going out the door in almost perfect shape every time.

"In contrast, Harley was experiencing quality problems to the tune of 30 percent, meaning that one out of three of their bikes needed to be fixed when it reached the end of the line. Combine their quality problems with an almost one-to-ten supervisor/manager-to-worker ratio and a bloated quality department of nearly thirty people where nothing ever went out on time, and even a blind man could see the contrast.

"So Harley management went back to their plant and changed everything. Why? Because they now knew what was possible. And the change was more than just abandoning systems and programs. It was really about what people could do. That was the biggest change. It was a change in thinking about people," said Kip.

"You're absolutely right," said Pete. "Several of my top executives own and ride Harleys. But they talk about how in the seventies, Harley-Davidson motorcycles ran poorly and leaked oil. What exactly did they do to turn the company around?"

"Well, under the leadership of CEO Vaughn Beals, Harley began a transformation up out of the red ink and back to a reputation for producing the finest motorcycles in the world," said Kip. "And they didn't do it in the traditional way of turning a company around by imposing new control-based management systems.

"Instead, they started by asking the people who produced the motorcycles what they thought the company should do. Management listened to the workers and turned control of the systems over to them. By instituting a freedom-based work environment that said 'Trust the workers completely,' the turnaround has been nothing short of spectacular!" Pete nodded.

"Harley-Davidson has experienced fifteen consecutive years of record revenue earnings. In fact, I saw that they finished the year with a total return of over 24 percent![1] And they're not the only ones who've enjoyed that kind of financial success using a freedom-based approach.

"Harley modestly cut back the quality group from almost thirty people to one person in the early days. They realized that to create a quality bike they needed to make everyone a quality expert or, better said, a quality *owner* of their job. Building accountability could never have happened in the old days because it was the quality control department's job to define quality and to measure it. Now it was everyone's job."

"Those are impressive results," added Pete.

"Yes, they are. When given the freedom to be responsible, the people at Harley-Davidson created unique ways of organizing and governing themselves. In fact, once an organization has created a freedom-based work environment—one based on trust and freedom without control—I believe the possibilities are infinite. Just look at what free enterprise has done for new technology and innovation."

"But, Kip," argued Pete, "don't some people take advantage of the lack of controls in a freedom-based work environment?"

"Of course a few members of every staff take advantage of an open workplace," answered Kip. "I'm sure it even happened at Harley. But my experience suggests that only a small percentage of people take advantage of an open society. A society or an organization has the right to protect itself from lawbreakers. But neither a business nor a nation should compromise the freedoms of an open society to accommodate a few wrongdoers."

"You're starting to sound like a politician," said Pete smiling.

Kip returned Pete's smile. "I believe it's the obligation of a freedom-based organization to create an environment where people have the opportunity to be responsible for making their own choices and to be accountable for their own results. That's what creating an adult environment is all about. It is an environment with choices, and I'd venture to bet that in the old days at Harley the workers didn't have any choices. What they had were control-based systems that said, 'Trust the numbers, not the people!'"

"Well, that sounds good for Harley or for National Stores," said Pete, "but is that approach really practical for every company and organization?"

"It's very practical," responded Kip, "but as I said, you have to change your beliefs about people to make this approach work. You've got to believe that people really can be trusted and really want to be great. In contrast, control-based thinking believes that people cannot be trusted and without controls in place, will perform poorly, take advantage—or worse.

"If you want to know how inefficient control-based thinking is, just take a look at the 80-to-20 rule. The rule goes like this, and it's prevalent in all industries: 'Twenty percent of the people do 80 percent of the work.' That's not too different from your own experience, is it, Pete? But in a freedom-based workplace, 95 percent of the people become fully engaged. That's the new rule!"

Pete, still not convinced, responded with another question. "So, are you suggesting that control-based management systems are to blame for a lack of accountability and that poor performance is a consequence of not trusting people?"

"I sure am," shot Kip right back. "In fact, I'll take the risk of adding that as long as an organization tries to control people with the latest control-based fad, its hope for sustained success is doomed!"

"Kip, I'd like to trust my people," said Pete, "but I find that some are always bending or breaking our company rules, so we have to keep adding new ones.

"That sadly seems to be the pattern almost everywhere," Kip acknowledged. "About 5 percent don't make it in a freedom-based workplace. But remember, that's one heck of a lot better than your alternative where 80 percent don't take responsibility."

But why set up new rules that penalize everyone for the failures or sins of the few? Why build control-based systems to safeguard the operation from the actions of a few untrustworthy people and in the process discourage your most creative people from generating the big wins?

Kip went to his more salient point. "But why set up new rules that penalize everyone for the failures or sins of the few? Why build control-based systems to safeguard the operation from the actions of a few untrustworthy people and in the process discourage your most creative people from generating the big wins?"

Pete listened intently as Kip made his points. "It's ironic when I think about it now in my own operation," admitted Pete, "but putting new rules in place probably sent the message that no one was to be trusted."

"Precisely!" said Kip. "Control-based thinking says that controls establish accountability. But freedom-based thinking says that controls stifle accountability and that only by trusting people will accountability become a reality.

"Frankly, Pete, you ultimately have to make a choice. You can't straddle the fence on this basic issue. Either you trust the people around you, or eventually you'll face what I faced that fateful Monday morning many years ago.

"I also learned that everyone will be looking at you to see if you really mean what's coming out of your mouth. Don't expect that just because you said it once people will believe you. No, you have to say it over and over again in lots of different ways. Pete, expect that your credibility will be tested. Mine was, and so was that of every manager and supervisor at National Stores. People want to know if your walk and your talk are consistent. If they aren't, they'll tell you soon enough."

Control-based thinking says that controls establish accountability. But freedom-based thinking says that control stifles accountability and that only by trusting people will accountability become a reality.

Both men sat lost in their own thoughts about the fragility of credibility.

After a moment Kip continued. "The basis of the freedom-based approach is to trust people completely, and you must refuse to place controls on them as a matter of principle and practicality. If a few individuals prove to be untrustworthy or unwilling to be accountable for both their performance and behavior, they simply can't stay.

"In my experience, I've found that the vast majority of people can be trusted and appreciate being treated with trust, and that a freedom-based environment is the best way to achieve sustainable results. When people are invited to own their job, you'd be surprised at the results you'll get."

Pete was silent for a moment, then looked at Kip and said, "If you've got concrete proof, then I'm all ears! But this leap of faith you're asking me to take is asking a lot."

"I know it is!" Kip looked at his watch and added with a wink, "If we keep talking like this, we're going to talk ourselves right out of lunch—something I rarely do." The two men stood up, stepped out into the corridor, and walked toward the dining car.

Pete wasn't convinced, and he wasn't about to accept anything Kip had said on faith alone. But in the relaxed atmosphere of the train, Pete was enjoying the conversation, and if nothing else, Kip was making an interesting argument.

As the two men made their way toward the dining car, Pete thought, "I haven't been on a train since my wife and I toured Europe." At the time, he was a penniless graduate student and his wife was a microbiologist at the Rockefeller Institute in New York City. Looking back on it now, their early years together were some of his happiest. Money wasn't the barometer then, and his future seemed full of hope.

Now he faced an unknown future. When he got back to corporate headquarters, he needed to produce results, and he knew that the new CFO would welcome any stumbling on his part. The irony was that the very systems he'd put in place were now the enemy to the very changes he was hearing he needed to make.

4

Do Incentives Really Motivate People? Or Are They Just a Quick Fix?

The dining car was crowded and noisy. Some travelers, packed into the booths, were engaged in lively conversations as they ate. Other more solitary passengers were reading newspapers or tapping the keys of their laptop computers as they dined quietly at the tables.

In the near corner was a tall, overweight man in an expensive-looking suit talking on his cell phone through the earpiece attachment. Chomping on an unlit cigar, he spoke loudly enough for the entire car to hear his end of the conversation. "I don't care what they *prefer*!" shouted the man in a mocking tone. "Ship them what we've got in stock. Besides, it's near the end of the month, and we've got a quota to meet!" He muttered to himself, "I'm surrounded by whining idiots. Why can't they think on their own? Do I have to tell them everything?"

Pete stopped and looked at the man. Inwardly he was embarrassed for both of them. What the man was saying was what Pete had often thought after he'd had a conversation with one of his people. Slowly he and Kip made their way past this man and down the length of the dining car. Waiters darted around them, taking orders and delivering food. The only two remaining seats were in a booth occupied by two women at the far end of the car. Kip and Pete walked over to the booth and asked if they could share the table.

The first woman looked to be in her mid-thirties and introduced herself. "Hi, I'm Lucy Woo. I just sat down myself. Please, join us."

The second woman, who looked to be in her early forties, had been silent up until now. Smiling, she said, "I'm Yolanda Worthington. This train was my only way out of Denver." Kip smiled, and Pete extended his hand and introduced himself and Kip.

After settling into their seats, Pete said, "This is my first time on this train. Is the food any good?"

Lucy replied, "I enjoyed breakfast this morning, but lunch should be an adventure." Everyone laughed politely. She went on, having scored some points with her audience. "I came into the dining car just a moment ago myself, and Yolanda was kind enough to allow me to sit with her. How about you two gentlemen—do you work together?"

"We're sharing a compartment, but we met just a couple of hours ago," answered Pete. "I'm the CEO of an optic systems company, and Kip is a retired CEO who helps organizations create what he calls a freedom-based work environment. Kip was telling me that creating a freedom-based work environment is the best way to get people to be accountable, and I had just asked him for proof."

"Well, I certainly understand the importance of getting people to be accountable," commented Yolanda. "As an incentive and compensation design specialist for a national organization out of Minneapolis, I've found that the best way to get people to be accountable is to structure compensation and incentive systems that motivate them. I'm not trying to drum up any business—" everyone laughed, "—but I really believe this, and I have lots of proof that incentives definitely work!"

Turning directly to Kip, Yolanda said, "I'm afraid I don't know what you mean by a freedom-based work environment. In fact, freedom and accountability don't seem to be in the same universe. Too much freedom can lead to anarchy. Accountability, on the other hand, means that you're obliged to others to meet your commitments, something I strongly believe in. So if I'm right, how do you get these two ideas to fit together?"

Pete was glad they had sat down at this table because he recognized that Yolanda was going to give Kip a run for his money. He sat back and waited for Kip's response. He didn't have to wait long.

"Let me see if I can explain," smiled Kip, welcoming the question. "A freedom-based work environment is one that has abandoned the idea of controlling or manipulating people." Kip took an especially long time drawing out the words 'manipulating people' so that Lucy, Pete, and Yolanda could read his conversational thrust. "Rather, a freedom-based environment trusts people to make good choices. Of course every operation needs standards.

"Take Southwest Airlines, considered the best-run and the most profitable major airline in this country. What is it that they have going for them? Good processes and systems, of course, but their competitive advantage is their people. Instead of controlling people, Southwest encourages their people to be creative and to own their jobs. They emphasize a freedom-based philosophy."

"With all due respect, Kip," broke in Lucy, "I completely disagree! I work in Chicago as an organizational development specialist with a large national consulting firm, and I believe it's processes we should trust and the numbers they generate, not people. Not that people are evil or anything, just that they need help—guidance and supervision."

"Boy," thought Pete, "this is too good to be true. Lucy and Yolanda are going to tag-team poor old Kip just like they do in pro wrestling." As much as he had taken an immediate liking to Kip, Pete realized this conversation would be valuable in two ways. First, these ladies weren't going to just accept what Kip had to say without a fight. And it already appeared that their comments and questions would help Pete formulate his thinking. Second, if by some chance Pete embraced Kip's philosophy, the younger man knew that there would be plenty of Lucys and Yolandas back at corporate, so this would be good hands-on practice identifying and fielding objections.

Lucy brought Pete's wandering mind back to the conversation when she said, "Without good solid systems and controls in place, too many things can go wrong—and if something can go wrong, it will. My experience suggests that getting out of a fix takes a lot more energy than what it took to get into it in the first place."

Lucy realized that she was monopolizing the conversation and said, "I'd like to make one last point if I may." The group nodded. "The problem, as I see it, is that managers too often chase after popular management fads that make big promises but don't deliver. But good solid systems and procedures will always be needed even with freedom-based systems." Pete appreciated Lucy's argument. It was the argument that he had made to Kip earlier.

Kip replied, "You're right, Lucy. One of the problems of human nature is that people tend to adopt popular ideas largely because others have already done so, and this couldn't be truer than with popular management fads. Despite the absence of data to support a new fad, many conclude that if it's popular, it must work!"

Yolanda wasn't quite sure where this was all leading. Pete was sitting back, enjoying the discourse. But Lucy, fully engaged in her conversation with Kip, looked like a cat ready to pounce on her prey.

Lucy, quick to respond, said, "That's precisely my point. That's why I spend my time on systems and processes that can be measured rather than waste my time dealing with people issues. It's bottom-line results I'm interested in, not hopes, promises, and soft, squishy guru stuff!" Yolanda continued to listen with interest because she was not sure whether Lucy would support her approach.

"I'm interested in results, too," agreed Kip. "Organizations today continue to implement a dizzying array of management fads. Often, management gurus ride into town like old Wild West medicine pitchmen offering a cure-all from the back of their covered wagons. But the solutions they offer are the same old formulas wrapped in attractive new packages.

"Lucy, I think we'd all agree that appropriate systems and procedures make sense. What I'm saying is that you can't ignore people, while focusing on systems and processes, and expect them to be accountable. Systems are only tools; like a seat belt, you have to be willing to wear it for it to do any good."

"You can say that again," echoed Pete.

Yolanda interjected, "Kip, I still don't quite understand what you're pitching."

Kip did not take offense at Yolanda's rather caustic comment. "Let me see if I can make myself clear," he continued. "Individuals are very special, perhaps unique, and as such, they're not predictable, so one system doesn't fit all situations. Yet human nature drives us all. Much of popular thinking about managing and motivating people is rooted in early twentieth-century theories of human behavior. And these early theories suggest that humans are capable of being programmed. I know lots of advertising guys who, on the one hand, believe a campaign is going to work because of the pretesting they've done, only to find a wildcat firefight on their hands from an unpredictable segment of the audience. As much as we'd like to believe we can control people's behaviors, in truth we can't."

Kip's audience was listening intently, even Yolanda, as he made his point clearer. "Harvard psychologist B. F. Skinner published a behaviorist theory of human motivation in 1938. His theory was based on what he called 'operant conditioning.'[1] His work was so well received that his approach has remained in our consciousness even to this day. For many of us, his theories—and they are only theories—have become our belief system about how to control and motivate people."

"I remember reading about him in my psychology classes at Penn," said Lucy.

Kip went on. "Operant conditioning asserts that an action may be controlled by a stimulus that comes after it rather than before it. Skinner's theories of human motivation have since been proven ineffective and even damaging to individuals and organizations. And yet people continue to try to apply his theories." He knew that Yolanda would hit the roof on his last point, but he felt compelled to lay out the facts.

There was no smile on Yolanda's face as she said, "You're talking about my business. The basis of our work and credibility is on the excellent science that Dr. Skinner pioneered. You can't be saying incentives don't work!" She was visibly upset by this stranger's assertions. "We've been helping companies encourage better individual performance for years, and we wouldn't still be in business if this *theory*, as you call it, didn't work! The incentive industry is a multibillion-dollar industry. That has to count for something!"

Kip listened patiently, letting Yolanda make her case to the other parties at the table. "Yolanda, I mean you or your industry no disrespect, but let me finish my point. Skinner believed that when a reward, or 'reinforcement,' follows a behavior, that behavior is likely to be repeated. And because Skinner was able to influence the behavior of laboratory rats and pigeons by feeding them when their behavior was 'correct,' he concluded that human beings are motivated in the same way!"

"Wait a minute—are you comparing people to rats and pigeons?" challenged Yolanda.

From Pete's corner of the table, he could see the fire darting out of Yolanda's eyes and was glad that her wrath was pointed at Kip and not him. He thought, "I hope my folks don't go nuclear on me if I bring these ideas back to them!" Then he turned toward Kip to fully catch his response.

Kip responded in a measured tone. "I'm not comparing people to rats—but our friend Skinner did." Lucy, enjoying the exchange, gave out a little laugh at Kip's last comment. If she was keeping score in her mind, it was one point for the old guy and goose egg for the incentive specialist.

He went on slowly and purposefully. "Most of what is commonly believed about human motivation and human nature is influenced, if not shaped, by his theories of nearly sixty-five years ago. Skinner's fingerprints can be seen literally everywhere in American society—in the business community, in our schools, in our churches, and even in our families. It's not these institutions, but behaviorist theory that is failing us."

Yolanda knew she was on the defensive, but she'd be darned if she would give an inch. "When I studied behaviorism in college, I accepted it as a fact, not a theory. And I don't remember anyone disputing his experiments or methodology."

"I, too, accepted his theories as fact," continued Kip, "and I went to school a long time before you did. This idea of offering rewards to motivate behavior became the bedrock of twentieth-century American management systems, and while I was a CEO, I used his approach all the time, not only at work but at home. Yet I now recognize that Skinner was mistaken. Contemporary researchers—those of the last thirty years—consider Skinner's work to be narrow in perspective and biased. But, Yolanda, they haven't gotten the publicity that Skinner has.

"Skinner made a contribution, but his work was just a single step in understanding human behavior, not the final word, as many would have us believe. Yolanda, it comes down to whether you believe that human behavior can be equated to that of pigeons and rats and can then make the leap to a belief that humans can be conditioned using Skinner's techniques."

Yolanda was silent. She crossed her arms and shook her head in disbelief. This stranger was attacking her basic beliefs. As the silence built, she racked her brain for a way to tell him he was wrong. She would've loved to have had her boss sitting at the table to argue her points more forcefully.

Pete offered a compromise position, trying to support Yolanda's argument. "So, if what you're telling us is true, why are incentives still so popular?"

"They're popular," replied Kip, "because offering incentives provides an easy answer to the problem of motivating people.

"I think that the North American culture, as opposed to our Asian and European counterparts, is steeped in behaviorism. From the time children enter the American public school system, they're indoctrinated in behaviorist thinking. Rather than appealing to the intrinsic learning motivators— the pure internal joy of learning, for example—students are offered stickers, stars, certificates, awards, trophies, and, most of all, grades as inducements to learn and to achieve."

Pete added enthusiastically, "Oh, boy, how true. But, you know, my wife and I tried to use stickers with our daughter, but she wouldn't have any part of it." He smiled to himself. "In fact, when she was in the third grade, my wife tried to make a deal with our daughter and said, 'If you make your bed, I'll put a gold star on the refrigerator.' And do you know what my daughter said? 'Mommy, if you want the gold star, you make my bed!'" Kip and Lucy laughed; Yolanda pursed her lips, looking uncomfortable and a little embarrassed. Pete realized that he had just scored some more points for Kip and felt badly for Yolanda, who seemed more out in the cold than ever.

"The incentive business," said Kip, "an entire industry based on the concept of rewards, is very much alive and well in America. Yolanda's industry is evidence of that fact. Most people are unaware, however, that behaviorist theory does not acknowledge such basic intrinsic motivators as personal accomplishment, thoughts, or feelings." Kip was trying to be as diplomatic as he could.

"That's not true!" shot back Yolanda, her voice rising. "Our incentive programs are designed specifically to appeal to an employee's sense of accomplishment. And there's nothing like additional cash in your pocket or a gift to reinforce that sense of accomplishment."

Kip responded calmly and in a low voice, "Everyone likes more money, Yolanda, but offering incentives allows management to ignore the real reasons behind poor performance. Rather than going through the hard work of finding the cause of low achievement, offering an incentive takes the easier road to inducing the behaviors the organization desires."

"Personally, I've never believed in incentives," interjected Lucy in an almost dismissive tone. It was apparent from her comment that she wasn't interested in being diplomatic or in pulling her punches and that she welcomed this conversation, even if it was getting a little uncomfortable for Yolanda. "As I said, I think you need to concentrate on the processes, not the people, if you want to see results. At best, incentives are the icing and not the cake."

"Looking at processes is certainly part of the answer, Lucy," responded Kip, trying to save the situation for Yolanda. "But without the enthusiastic involvement of the people using the processes, nothing positive happens on a sustainable basis."

"That's precisely why incentives help," interjected Yolanda. "Yeah, they might be the icing, but don't most people eat the cake for the icing?" She sat back in her seat, confident that she'd made an important point.

"It would seem so at one level," smiled Kip, "but I would suggest that there's a mountain of evidence that catalogues the disastrous long-term effects of reward systems as a primary driver of behavior as would a diet of straight sugar."

Pete broke in with a wry smile. "Maybe too much icing spoils the experience of eating the cake!" He raised his eyebrows quizzically, his eyes darting toward Lucy's. As she glanced back, their eyes connected briefly in conspiratorial amusement.

"Highly regarded incentive systems," continued Kip, as gently as he could, "such as pay-for-performance and merit pay—in short, any and all motivational systems that seek to manipulate the behavior of others through extrinsic motivators—are born of Skinner's theories. Each of these strategies puts into practice the belief that motivation is something that gets done *to* others."

"My experience tells me that you can motivate people with incentives," countered Yolanda defensively. "Most of the executives I work with find that offering the right incentives, if they are structured properly, encourages their people to conquer challenges and meet goals. That's where our company can help them and why we are so successful."

Kip paused and spoke in a lower tone of voice. "But modern researchers conclude that following this path has extracted a heavy toll."

Lucy could see that Kip was whispering into the wind with Yolanda, yet Kip continued with great patience. "Now, here's my point. If the incentives don't work, most executives assume their people are to blame. It never occurs to them that the manipulative nature of incentive plans is really to blame. And, with all due respect, that's where our greatest disagreement is centered."

Yolanda, clearly upset, spoke slowly in a controlled tone. "Kip, you're making a lot of claims without offering any evidence to back them up. Unless you can prove what you're saying, I've heard quite enough."

"I'd be glad to show you proof. Give me a moment to get my briefcase from my compartment, and I'll share the proof with you all."

Just then, the waiter appeared. "What can I get you for lunch today? Have you had enough time to look over the menu?"

They each quickly glanced at the menu and ordered, and then Kip excused himself to retrieve his briefcase. As he moved away from the table, he couldn't help noticing that the big man in the corner with the unlit cigar in his mouth was again giving someone the worst of his temper on his cell phone.

Kip shook his head and opened the dining car door.

5

Is Job Security Related to a Corporate Culture's Bottom Line?

The four strangers had lost some of their earlier mystery as their opinions began to unfold. When Kip returned, Pete said, "Kip, I've been thinking about our incentive plans, and I've got to tell you that I agree with Yolanda. For at least some of my people, the pay-for-performance plans have worked well. In fact, one or two of my salespeople earn more than I do." Lucy laughed, and Kip seemed sincerely interested in Pete's point. Yolanda, on the other hand, had been burnt before by these three and was sitting in a more wait-and-see posture.

"There are always individuals in any organization, public or private, who possess hard-wired advantages like intelligence, charm, or cunning to exploit these programs," Kip granted. "They're able to make virtually any incentive program work to their advantage. These individuals consistently win the contests and earn the incentive pay that seems to elude their peers. Proponents of incentive pay plans argue that money motivates! And they're right—but only to a point."

"OK, Kip, so where's your proof?" asked Pete, offering support to Yolanda's cause.

"Well, first, let me relate a story, and then I'll share some facts to back it up," said Kip.

"A good friend of mine was a division manager in the mid-seventies at Avon Corporation, the cosmetic giant. One year the annual winter sales competition was won by one of the district sales managers in his division. Let's call her Mrs. Brown.

"At the close of the contest, my friend received a call from a representative of another district in his division alleging that Mrs. Brown had cheated by falsifying orders. When he investigated, my friend found that Mrs. Brown had opened the sealed envelopes containing her representative's sales orders and had increased reported sales to exceed her district's quota. By manipulating the orders, Mrs. Brown had won the sales contest by a wide margin. She had deluded herself into believing that cheating was justified in order to win the contest. Ultimately, what she won was a thirty-day suspension without pay and disgrace among her peers.

"Here was a loyal, hard-working woman who had, in her own mind, believed that because of the pressure she was under, doing whatever it took to win the contest was OK. But, by cheating, she had squandered her reputation and the trust of her staff.

"So, who's accountable in this situation—Mrs. Brown or the organization?" asked Kip.

"Mrs. Brown cheated," answered Yolanda. "She was accountable because she had to know that what she did was wrong. And you can't blame the incentive program; this was an issue of character."

"I think both Mrs. Brown and the company were accountable," responded Kip. "When she was confronted, Mrs. Brown admitted that she had cheated, and she knew it was wrong. But the research I'll share with you in a moment indicates that the organization was also accountable because the incentive program itself created the conditions that seduced Mrs. Brown to cheat. No, that doesn't get Mrs. Brown off the hook. But why place anyone in this position when you don't really need to?

"And let's not forget that in that division alone there were seventeen other sales managers who were affected by this competitive environment. And, yes, they didn't cheat, but they paid a price—just not with a suspension. And when you include the over 180 sales representatives in each district, there were lots of people touched by this contest and its long-term effects."

"Well, you're right there, Kip, but getting back to Mrs. Brown, how can you assert in any way that the incentive program was responsible for her cheating?" countered Pete.

"Yeah!" chimed in Lucy, vigorously shaking her head in agreement.

And Yolanda? Well, Yolanda was just short of jumping up and storming off. The audacity of this man, blaming a program for what was clearly an ethics issue!

"I wouldn't have related this story, Pete, if Mrs. Brown's behavior wasn't typical of what often happens with incentive programs," answered Kip. "What each of you is going to have to decide is whether we have lots of immoral folks working for us or whether it just might be the context of the incentive programs themselves that causes this kind of unprincipled behavior again and again. Research shows—and not from only a single source—that contests and incentives are a cause of both low motivation and a wide range of undesirable behaviors, including cheating.

"More important, the research also pinpoints that the use of extrinsic motivators such as contests damages an individual's intrinsic motivation, inhibits the personal will to succeed, and destroys the pure joy of a job well done."

"*Come on!*" exclaimed Yolanda, visibly incensed. Not only did she not believe a word of what this man was saying, but his comments directly affronted the underpinnings of everything she believed about the value of her career.

Lucy, turning to Yolanda, interrupted. "In all fairness, Mr. Kiplinger is not spouting off. I've read articles in some of the leading business journals that directly challenge incentive programs. I'm not convinced myself of what Kip is saying, but I think we need to hear him out."

"Here's the evidence that supports my point." Kip reached into his briefcase and withdrew a large manila folder. A University of Rochester professor of psychology and director of the Human Motivation Program, Edward L. Deci, Ph.D., wrote a book on the subject of human motivation entitled *Why We Do What We Do.* In it, he sheds light on the destructive power of offering money and rewards to encourage desired behaviors." Kip began reading out loud from the folder.

> Obviously, money constitutes a powerful force. Certainly there can be no doubt that it motivates. One need only look around even at oneself to see how willing people are to engage in a wide range of activities for money. They get hooked on gambling, sometimes losing everything they own, because of the irrational belief that they will hit the big one. They take on extra assignments that unduly stress them, perhaps to the point of making them sick, because of the extra money. And they engage in a wide variety of nefarious activities that promise handsome rewards. Sure, money motivates, but that's not the point. The point is that while money is motivating people, it is also undermining their intrinsic motivation and . . . [incentives have] a variety of other negative effects as well.[1]

"You keep talking about negative effects!" persisted Yolanda, again feeling overwhelmed and attacked.

"OK," said Kip. "Alfie Kohn, a prolific author on the negative effects of incentives, puts it this way: 'Do rewards motivate people? Absolutely! They motivate people to get rewards'[2]—regardless of what it takes to get them," he added. "Here's a short list of some of the studies Kohn cites in his book *Punished by Rewards,* documenting the negative effects of extrinsic motivators." At that, Kip slid a sheet across the table for his companions to view:

- Curry, Susan J., Edward H. Wagner, and Louis C. Grothaus. "Intrinsic and Extrinsic Motivation for Smoking Cessation." *Journal of Educational Research* 68 (1975).

- Dickenson, Alyce M. "The Detrimental Effects of Extrinsic Reinforcement on 'Intrinsic Motivation.'" *The Behavior Analyst* 12 (1989).

- Dienstbier, Richard A., and Gary K. Leak. "Overjustification and Weight Loss: The Effects of Monetary Reward." Paper presented at the annual convention of the American Psychological Association, Washington, D.C., September 1976.

- Geller, E. Scott, Michael J. Kalsher, James R. Rudd, and Galen R. Lehman. "Promoting Safety Belt Use on a University Campus: An Integration of Commitment and Incentive Strategies." *Journal of Applied Social Psychology* 19 (1989).

- Kadzin, Alan E., and Richard R. Bootzin. "The Token Economy: An Evaluative Review." *Journal of Applied Behavior Analysis* 5 (1972).

- Thorne, Paul. "Fitting Rewards." *International Management* 88 (December 1990).

"That's an interesting list. But can you summarize the points all these studies make—if there's a common thread?" inquired Pete.

Yolanda was beginning to feel like she was standing in front of a firing squad and didn't know whether she could continue to take the bullets she was experiencing. She sincerely believed she was doing something important in her work, and now this man was telling her that she has been dishing out poison to her clients. Her clients respected her and, in general, liked the results they'd experienced from working with her. How could this be bad?

Kip pulled out another sheet. "Pete, here are some of the documented adverse side effects of extrinsic motivators found in these and other studies."

Negative Effects of Extrinsic Motivation

- Resistance to new ideas
- Resentment
- A lack of personal engagement
- A sense of alienation and hopelessness

- Behavior inconsistent with personal values
- An inability to regulate behavior because of fear
- Outright defiance and rebellion
- Self-destructive behavior
- Narcissism
- Self-imposed isolation
- Cheating
- Lying
- Diminished interest
- A sense of victimization
- Disrespect for authority
- Low self-esteem
- Lack of autonomy
- Childish behaviors
- Low-quality work
- A sense of entitlement

After passing the list to the others, Pete responded, "OK, everyone knows that money is a powerful motivator—no one would disagree with that. But I still can't see how offering money or rewards creates all these negative side effects."

"Neither can I!" added Yolanda indignantly. Lucy was now more on Kip's side than on Yolanda's because Lucy had seen firsthand how overdoing incentives can ultimately destroy a person's motivation.

"Let me see if I can explain." Kip pondered for a moment and then continued. "Over the past several decades, researchers have begun to explore the multifaceted subject of intrinsic motivation, a subject that has been mostly ignored in the private sector. Psychologists, psychiatrists, philosophers, theologians, and statesmen have expounded on the quantifiable benefits of intrinsic motivation—the inner joy of accomplishment. Intrinsic motivators have been shown to enhance self-esteem and improve performance enormously."

"We're not going to get a sermon on self-esteem now, are we?" interjected Lucy in a sarcastic tone. Pete and Kip laughed. Yolanda didn't budge.

"No, no sermon," responded Kip, still smiling.

Pete looked at the older man and recognized that Kip had a passion for the subject but didn't take himself too seriously. He recognized that that was one of Kip's qualities that made him so easy to listen to and believe.

Continuing, Kip said, "In fact, although the research I've cited documents the advantages of intrinsic motivation over extrinsic motivation, there is also a downside." Yolanda was glad that Kip was a big enough individual to admit that his theory had a hole in it, too.

"Relying on intrinsic motivation to improve performance takes a great deal of time, patience, and commitment," said Kip. That wasn't exactly the kind of backtracking Yolanda was prepared to hear.

"In this fast-paced business world," Pete challenged, "isn't that asking a lot from CEOs and senior executives who need to show results immediately? Personally, I don't have the luxury of time to build an environment of intrinsic motivation; plus, it sounds a little airy-fairy to me."

Pete had just made the argument that Kip heard repeatedly from new clients. "Pete, when you say you don't have the luxury of time to create intrinsic motivation," asked Kip with a deliberate tone, "aren't you really asking whether spending your time on building intrinsic motivation is worth the investment in the long term? Isn't this really an issue of creating long-term value for your organization?"

"I suppose it is," agreed Pete in a thoughtful tone. "When it comes right down to it, I'd do almost anything, as long as it was ethical, to build the long-term value of my company. In fact, that's exactly what our stockholders expect of me as the CEO."

"Right, and they should," concurred Kip. "A significant amount of data gathered over the past thirty years strongly indicates that corporate cultures that rely on extrinsic motivation do not sustain organizational performance as well as those that rely on intrinsic motivation, and some even break the law in their attempt to make their numbers.

"And a word on the airy-fairy stuff you talked about." Kip smiled at Pete. "In my experience the soft stuff is really the hard stuff when you get down to it. The research also indicates that it's the soft stuff that makes the biggest difference to an operation's bottom-line results.

"Now, I realize that a lot of professional business managers might not agree with that statement," Kip winked at Lucy when he said this, "until they see the numbers Professor Kotter and others have accumulated over the past many years. Once they see the numbers though, it's hard to dispute the research."

Yolanda, Lucy, and Pete listened intently as Kip continued.

Kip pulled another folder from his briefcase and withdrew a sheet of paper. "In their book *Corporate Culture and Performance*, Harvard professors John Kotter and James Heskett discuss the link between culture and long-term profits. Here's what they conclude: 'The culture issue may even be greater than all [the] other factors combined.' And when I say culture, I'm really talking about the contrast in beliefs and responses to business issues between control-based and freedom-based operations.

"I'm going to simplify this using a graphic. The 'C' signifies a culture that's control-based, and an 'F' defines a culture that is freedom-based. So the question that Professors Kotter and Heskett are talking about contrasts the two. Which culture, C or F, is the most efficient and effective? The numbers seem to speak for themselves." At this point Kip drew a simple graphic.

Lucy shook her head. "You're telling me that the factors of how companies execute their enterprise-wide strategy, design their organizational structure, craft their management systems, and establish their financial tools, along with how effective their leadership is, are less important than the organization's culture?" she asked in disbelief.

"Yes, that's what Kotter and Heskett's research concludes," said Kip. "And continual examples in the newspaper week after week of failed organizations that lose the trust of

the marketplace center around the fundamental differences of control versus freedom—C versus F. I believe Kotter and Heskett's comments state the obvious. Here, listen to what they say." Kip read from the paper he now held:

- **Corporate culture can have a significant impact on a firm's long-term economic performance.** Firms with cultures that emphasized all the key managerial constituencies (customers, stockholders, and employees) and leadership from managers at all levels outperformed firms that did not have those cultural traits by a wide margin.

- **Corporate culture will probably be an even more important factor in determining the success or failure of firms in the next decade.** In a world that is changing at an increasing rate, one would predict that unadaptive cultures ["C" cultures] have an even larger negative financial impact.

- **Corporate cultures that inhibit strong long-term financial performances are not rare; they develop easily, even in firms that are full of reasonable and intelligent people.** Companies that encourage inappropriate behavior and inhibit change to more appropriate strategies tend to emerge slowly and quietly over a number of years. ["C" cultures tend to be resistant to change.]

- **Although tough to change, corporate cultures can be made more performance enhancing.** Such change is complex, takes time, and requires leadership, which is different from even excellent management.[3] [It's the culture C or F that makes the biggest difference, not leadership.]

"There's nothing in those points that discounts the effectiveness of incentives," Yolanda said triumphantly, rejecting Kip's thesis. "In fact, I'd argue that offering incentives is a contributing factor to building a productive corporate culture."

"That's true," replied Kip. "These excerpts, although they stress the importance of corporate culture, don't specify what kind of culture is best. So, if we agree with Kotter and Heskett's conclusion—that culture influences financial performance—then the question is, 'What kind of corporate culture sustains improvements in performance?'"

Lucy broke in, "That's one of my questions too, Kip. What kind of corporate culture best supports financial results? And I'm specifically referring to shareholder value."

"OK, Lucy, let's talk real shareholder value," responded Kip patiently, while reaching for another folder. "In their book *Built to Last: Successful Habits of Visionary Companies*, James Collins and Jerry Porras of Stanford University examined eighteen exceptional companies to find out why they outperformed their competitors." Kip scanned a page he had just pulled from his folder as he spoke. "All eighteen were premier institutions in their respective industries with up to one hundred years in business, and all had outperformed the stock market by a factor of fifteen times since 1926."[4]

"Their stock performance is certainly impressive," commented Lucy. "But Pete asked about which culture, C or F, delivers the best bottom-line results, and I don't think you've answered his question yet."

"OK, let's talk about which produces the best bottom-line results," said Kip. "Here's what Collins and Porras found," and he read from his paper:

> First, they all had a solid foundation of shared values that had not changed to fit current fads. Second, making money was not their sole aim, but was balanced with other objectives like contributing to the good of the community. Third, they focused on continuous improvement as a key strategy. Fourth, they were open to experimentation and to learning from their own failures. Finally, they had highly adaptive cultures that enabled them to adjust constantly to change. Pete commented, "A highly adaptive culture is another way of saying a freedom-based culture or an 'F' operation."

Attributes of High-Performance Freedom-Based Operations

First, they all had a solid foundation of shared values that had not changed to fit current fads.

Second, making money was not their sole aim, but was balanced with other objectives like contributing to the good of the community.

Third, they focused on continuous improvement as a key strategy.

Fourth, they were open to experimentation and to learning from their own failures.

Fifth, they had highly adaptive cultures that enabled them to adjust constantly to change.

"Yes," nodded Kip. "Lucy and Pete, right now the focus in many corporate cultures is on so-called shareholder value. But what passes for shareholder value today, a quarter-by-quarter fixation on the bottom line, often mortgages the organization's financial future for short-term gains and sets back the ability of the organization to create long-term value. This thinking epitomizes classic control-based thinking."

"Those are pretty strong words. I'd like to see you back that up!" broke in Lucy. Pete nodded his head in agreement.

Kip withdrew yet another sheet from the folder. "Now I'm about to sound like a professor back at college," smiled Kip. Pete and Lucy laughed. "But you asked for proof, so here goes.

"In his book *The End of Shareholder Value*, Allan Kennedy writes about the effects of an obsession with the bottom line another form of 'C' organizational thinking." Having said that, Kip began to read from the paper he held:

The Contrast in Thinking

The actions of managers obsessed with the bottom line have truly devastated the cultures of most large corporations. . . . Making this community the workplace inviting to all employees, putting a meaningful human dimension back into it, is key to restoring an effective culture, which is in turn a proven way to guarantee long-term success.[5]

"Basically," Kip continued, "what Kennedy is saying is that a freedom-based organization, one that has a 'meaningful human dimension,' relies on intrinsic motivation rather than incentives and other extrinsic motivators. This is the key to creating an effective 'F' corporate culture."

"You still haven't given us the bottom-line results," challenged Pete in an almost terse tone.

Kip responded with a smile, "I'm getting there, Pete. When Collins and Porras compared adaptive cultures to nonadaptive cultures in *Built to Last*, the financial results were astounding! For instance, revenue growth over an eleven-year period in adaptive freedom-based cultures averaged 682 percent, while nonadaptive cultures or control-based 'C' operations averaged just 166 percent. In the same period, net income for adaptive cultures, 'F' operations, rose 756 percent, while nonadaptive cultures, 'C' businesses, eked out a measly 1 percent!"[6]

Kip paused to make sure that all three of his table-mates were ready for his final point. "These aren't just numbers. They relate to how people are treated and show that, if you treat people like adults—well, as you just heard, the results can be incredible."

Comparing Adaptive Cultures, "F" Operations, to Nonadaptive Cultures, "C" Businesses

- *Revenue Growth* over an eleven-year period
  —Adaptive cultures "F" averaged 682 percent
  —Nonadaptive cultures "C" averaged 166 percent

- *Net Income* in the same period
  —Adaptive cultures "F" up 756 percent
  —Nonadaptive cultures "C" up 1 percent![7]

"Now that's bottom-line results!" conceded Pete, his face alight with enthusiasm. Lucy gently pulled the paper from Kip's hand to review the findings and nodded in agreement. Yolanda appeared to be almost floating alone in her own world and didn't seem to be interested in the conversation.

"Yes, Pete," said Kip, "and the real bottom-line message is that building a freedom-based corporate culture equates not only to a better place to work but also to real long-term shareholder value and job security! So what's it to be: an 'F' approach or a 'C' approach?"

Yolanda finally interjected, "You still haven't made the connection between intrinsic motivation and a healthy corporate culture."

"That's a fair point, Yolanda." Kip hoped to make Yolanda a part of the discovery process instead of an adversary, and this was the opening he'd been waiting for.

"F" Cultures Generate the Big Bucks!

Building a freedom-based corporate culture equates not only to a better place to work but also to real long-term shareholder value and job security!

Kip reflected a moment and then said, "OK, let me see if I can do that. You've no doubt heard of the influential French philosopher Jean-Paul Sartre." He waited for Yolanda to respond before he began.

"Sure, who hasn't?" replied Yolanda.

"Well, Sartre set forth some really interesting ideas that are relevant to intrinsic motivation and a healthy social or corporate culture," continued Kip. "He believed that the bedrock of human existence and the foundation of intrinsic motivation is the freedom to choose. And that it's in choosing that we become truly accountable both to ourselves and to the community we live and work in. When people are given the freedom to choose, a healthy social or corporate culture is possible."

Pete loved to listen to Kip when he was on a roll. He continued to be amazed at how Kip had so many ideas and concepts at his fingertips.

"Furthering this point," declared Kip, "in 1968, noted psychological theoretician Richard deCharms published a very interesting book. He suggested that the key to intrinsic motivation lay in an individual's desire to be the origin of one's choices and actions. And that people resented being manipulated by other persons or external forces.[8] And, as I said earlier, a freedom-based culture promotes intrinsic motivation by giving people the freedom to make choices devoid of manipulation."

Kip had finished his point when Yolanda broke in. "Now that's another place where we differ. I don't think incentives are manipulative. I think they're inspiring to people," she said.

"I think I understand what you're saying to Yolanda," added Lucy, ignoring Yolanda's statement. Lucy wanted to focus the conversation on the importance of intrinsic motivation and didn't want to argue about whether incentives were manipulative or inspirational. She had already decided that Kip's information won the point and didn't want to get into an argument with Yolanda.

"Let me see if I can put it in my own words," Lucy said almost too enthusiastically. "In order to be intrinsically motivated, I must feel free to act because of the satisfaction or enjoyment I derive from the activity, not because management directives or incentives are causing me to act. Is that what you're saying?"

"Exactly!" exclaimed Kip. "For modern researchers, the choice is clear. Do organizations build an environment that depends primarily on rewards as extrinsic motivators—something that is very costly and not very effective. . . ." Pete glanced at Yolanda as Kip was speaking, knowing that Kip's comment would set Yolanda off again. ". . . Or do we take the time to build an environment that encourages intrinsic motivation based on what each individual finds personally motivating?"

"You're making a pretty strong argument," said Pete emphatically. "Getting people to become intrinsically motivated by giving them choices makes sense. But reality dictates that you can't give people unlimited choices."

"I agree," said Lucy.

"You're right," replied Kip, looking to both Pete and Lucy. "The key is to get people to acknowledge real limitations without abdicating their responsibility to make choices."

Leaning forward, Lucy said, "But isn't this where system controls come into play?"

Kip looked at Lucy and said, "Only when people begin making intelligent choices while taking into account the limitations do they begin to become accountable for their choices.

"Control systems allow people to cop out on accountability," he continued. "You hear people saying, 'I have no choice;

the system won't allow me to do anything else.' When this happens, you know people have become dependent on the system and, more important, will never become accountable. You often hear people ask, 'Who's accountable?' when what they really mean is, 'Who's to blame?'"

Yolanda saw another opening and took it. "I'd love to have a dollar for every comment I've received from a help desk person or salesperson or customer service person who has looked me in the eye and said, 'Sorry, but that's the policy. Personally I'd like to help you, but . . .'"

Interrupting, Pete said with a smile. "Yeah, that drives me crazy! Let me tell you all a quick story that emphasizes Yolanda's exact point.

"Recently, I had to get my passport renewed. It was still valid, but it would expire while I was overseas, so our travel agency suggested that I update it before I left so there wouldn't be a hassle when I returned home.

"My assistant, Pam, and I figured that we'd simply send in a couple of passport photos, and they would reissue my passport. We had about three weeks, so we felt there shouldn't be a problem in turning around this request. You're not going to believe what happened next!

"Pam called the local passport agency. Guess what? An answering machine told her that if we wanted to talk to a real live person, it would cost us thirty-five cents a minute."

Kip and Lucy chuckled and shook their heads in disbelief. "When Pam called back, the answering machine told her their hours and the directions to their office. It also indicated that the holder of the passport needed to come in personally.

"So I took off work to go down to their office. The place was almost vacant. I walked up to two guards who sat at their posts, slouching like they were watching a football game. As I approached, one of them said, 'Yes?' like I was interrupting him. I asked what the procedure was for renewing my passport, and the guard said that I needed to make an appointment.

"Now remember, this place is vacant except for one poor customer sitting in a chair. I hit the roof. I said, 'An appointment! Are you kidding? There isn't anyone here. Why can't I just go up to the window and get it processed?'

"'No,' said the guard, 'you can't do that.' Now, I'm an American citizen, and I pay *lots* of taxes. And here are these two guards doing nothing and the place is empty, and I'm being told I can't get this simple process started, that I need to make an appointment. I was upset and I was losing it— literally.

"I must have been making a lot of noise because a clerk from inside came up. He said that there was a phone on the wall I could use to make the appointment and that my assistant could come back and process my passport application. The attendant suggested that I write my congressman if I had a problem with this procedure. Can you believe it?

"So I called and made an appointment for later that day, even though I was catching a plane to Minneapolis in about an hour and a half and wouldn't be able to keep it myself. After all, the clerk had just said that my assistant could keep it, right?"

"What happened next?" asked Lucy, obviously having a ball with this story.

By this time, Kip was shaking his head in disbelief and openly laughing. Tears were forming in the corners of his eyes. Even Yolanda had to give some ground and smiled as Pete spun his tale.

"Well, when Pam arrived for the appointment," said Pete, she was promptly told that she was *not* the bearer of the passport so she couldn't apply."

"Incensed, Pam said, 'This is absolutely ridiculous! First, I can't get the information when I call. Then, you want to charge me thirty-five cents a minute to speak to a live person. Next, when we follow your instructions and Pete comes down here in person, he can't process his passport because he doesn't have an appointment, even though the place is empty. Then, he makes the appointment, and you tell him that it's OK to have his assistant keep the appointment, but when I come all the way down here, you tell me that I can't renew his passport because I'm not the bearer. This is crazy!'"

"The guard said he was sorry but that that was the policy. Pam was furious, to put it mildly."

"What did she do?" asked Kip, still laughing at the image of Pam and Pete being run around like that.

"Well, luckily," said Pete, "the same clerk heard what was going on, came up to her, and said she had remembered the 'wild man' from the morning."

At this point, all three members of the table were in stitches. Lucy and Yolanda were holding their sides, while Kip had tears streaming down his face. Pete really knew how to get the most out of a story.

Pete continued with a straight face. "The clerk was kind enough to shepherd Pam through the process, stating that they were making an exception in this case!"

"Absolutely unbelievable!" said Yolanda in an incredulous voice.

"Not as unbelievable as you might think," smiled Kip. "Some of you might remember the book *Catch 22*. In it, the Rule 22 stated that if you were in the service and were crazy, you could be honorably discharged."

"Yeah," said Pete, finishing Kip's thought, "and the catch-22 was that if you declared you were crazy, you obviously weren't."

They all laughed, but Lucy, feeling the heat of their jokes about systems, sat back and frowned.

"So, back to the subject," said Pete, straightening his posture and clearing his throat. "Kip, how do I set appropriate limits for my staff without being accused of controlling them?"

"That's a difficult question to answer, Pete," began Kip as he shifted in his seat, "mostly because it depends on how ready you are to give up control and how capable they are of making choices and being accountable for their choices. I think the two most important jobs of a leader in a freedom-based environment are to help people understand their choices and to create the conditions where people can grow to become accountable. Put another way, lead without ruling."

Pete thought a moment and then said, "I'm not sure if some of my people will ever be ready to be accountable."

Lucy nodded in agreement, while Yolanda stared out the window.

Kip responded, "In all seriousness, Pete, they'll never be ready to be accountable if they're not given the freedom to make choices. Granted, some of their choices will be the wrong ones, but that's a small price to pay considering the alternative."

That last remark seemed to stop the conversation for the moment, for the waiter had arrived with their lunch.

6

Do You Want to Be Controlled?

As lunch was served and the foursome shared a meal together, an undeclared truce allowed the conversation to turn to matters such as the snowstorm and the upcoming holiday season. Each member of the party told a funny story that kept the conversation flowing and drained away some of the earlier tension, though Yolanda was noticeably more subdued than the rest of the group. The train rumbled on as the wintry countryside, framed in the dining coach window, swiftly passed by.

Yolanda had been silent for quite some time. Finally, she let out a sigh, cleared her throat, and with a note of resignation said, "If you'll excuse me, please, I'd like to get back to my compartment. I've got some calls to make, and I need to write a few e-mails."

After she'd gone, Pete turned to Kip and said, "I guess you didn't convince her."

"No," said Kip with compassion in his voice, "not everyone will be open to accepting the possibility that incentives aren't the solution. It can take time to win them over. And, remember, she believes that incentives enrich a workplace. I just respectfully disagree with that position."

Just then a loud voice rose above the dining car. The cigar-chewing man in the corner shouted into his cell phone, "Hello, Mary, this is Hank Striker. My flight out of Denver was canceled by a snowstorm, so I'm on this blasted train that will arrive in L.A. at 6:30 in the morning on Thursday. Can you believe it? I'm going to be stuck on this tin can for two days! So I need you to reschedule today's and Wednesday's meetings for this Thursday."

Hank paused to listen a moment and in a loud, commanding voice said, "I don't care if the rest of them have to wait a day for me to get there. I'm the boss and I pay their salaries. They can wait—that's what I pay them to do!" There was another short pause. "That sounds fine, Mary. Oh, and tell Ted I don't want them sitting around the pool or playing golf; I want their behinds on the phone calling customers. We need another $2 million to meet this quarter's sales budget."

Pete couldn't help but overhear the man's rude comments. He thought about how when he was a young sales manager that he had worked for a great boss and had always been grateful that he never worked for a guy like this.

Pete brought the trio's attention back to their previous discussion with a comment: "Kip, if the business community ever accepted these ideas about freedom-based work environments, Yolanda's days as an incentive specialist would be numbered, and that joker in the back of the car would be out of a job."

"That's probably true about him," responded Kip with a chortle, "but Yolanda struck me as a bright and thoughtful woman. She may eventually embrace these new ideas. As more and more organizations catch on to the idea of a freedom-based work environment, there'll be a need for people with her experience and knowledge to help clients find creative ways to design freedom-based compensation plans. In a freedom-based world, restructuring compensation will be a big issue."

Pete added, "It sure would be a big issue in our organization." He paused to think for a moment and then said,

"Changing the subject, Kip, I'm really intrigued by your theories on freedom-based accountability, but I've still got lots of questions. Lucy, is it OK if I ask a few here?" Lucy smiled and nodded. She was enjoying the sharing of ideas and appreciated the stimulating discussion.

"I'm all yours," said Kip, putting down his fork.

"First of all," said Pete, "freedom is not a new idea. After all, the United States was founded on the principle of freedom. If the philosophy you espouse is so effective, why don't more American organizations follow it?"

Lucy added, "I'm interested in your response to that question, too."

"It's a good question," said Kip, "and, as you might imagine, I've given a lot of thought to why control-based management systems continue to be so popular in America. As I see it, since World War II, control-based management systems have moved through three distinct generations of management approaches and thinking.

"The first generation is the time-honored, top-down approach. This centuries-old approach controls people by limiting access to resources and information. And most operations that employ this approach employ directive leadership. Most executives who ascribe to this approach see it as the historic and optimal way to run an organization. But it's a leftover from the days of the tribal chiefs and kings, a time when concentrating power and control in the hands of a small number of powerful men was seen as their birthright."

The first generation is the time-honored, top-down approach. This centuries-old approach controls people by limiting access to resources and information and employing directive leadership.

"Well, if it's worked for centuries, there must be something good about it," interjected Lucy.

73

"Sure, it's worked," replied Kip. "It works as long as you have a steady supply of compliant, uneducated workers who'll do what they're told and leaders who are willing to make every decision and to control the information."

"But easy access to information in the Internet age and the need for speed," interrupted Pete, "and the rising expectations of a more educated workforce have changed things dramatically."

"And don't forget," chimed in Lucy, "women are now a key part of the workforce, and they aren't their mother's generation, either."

"You've got a point, Lucy," said Pete. Smiling, he glanced at Kip for agreement on that point.

Kip continued. "Next came the incentive-driven behaviorist approach, which we've just discussed with Yolanda. I call that the second generation. As the fifties and sixties created a growing middle-class in America with greater economic opportunity than ever before, offering incentives seemed the perfect solution for improving productivity and selling products. The incentive-driven approach tries to motivate people to be accountable by offering rewards to reinforce desired behaviors, but it's a misapplication of capitalism.

The second generation, the incentive-driven approach, tries to motivate people to be accountable by offering rewards to reinforce desired behaviors, but it's a misapplication of capitalism.

"Since incentive plans are often set up as internal competitions, they pit one worker or team against another. The theory is that competing for rewards will improve motivation and maximize utilization of resources. The reality is that internal competition leads to hoarding resources and withholding information for competitive advantage. It destroys trust between people. Additionally, most people believe they have no chance of winning the incentives and give up before the contest even begins."

"Boy, that's the truth!" chimed in Pete. "Our company has spent millions of dollars on incentives that didn't pay off. I didn't say that while Yolanda was here because I didn't want her to feel like we were ganging up on her."

"Well," said Lucy with a wink, "you have a strange way of pulling your punches!" The three people remaining at the table enjoyed poking fun at each other.

Kip laughed and continued. "More recently, the third generation, the conditional-freedom approach, has become very popular. This approach tries to make people more accountable by offering more freedom to those who 'deserve' it.

"Conditional freedom, Pete and Lucy, gives people freedom on the condition that they show personal improvement. In the end, this approach is nothing more than a more subtle form of the old carrot and stick. This strategy attempts to cause organizational change by first influencing attitudes and individual behavior."

The third generation, the conditional-freedom approach, tries to make people more accountable by offering more freedom to those who "deserve" it.

Kip shuffled through his folder again and withdrew an article. "This 1990 article absolutely blew my mind when I read it because a similar experience took place at National Stores. Pete, if you're considering changing your workplace, this is a must read. I bought a lot of copies for all my managers—that's how important I found it. So let me tell you the nugget of the piece.

"Professors Beer, Eisenstat, and Spector point out why trying to change people is a fundamentally flawed approach. Listen to what they say in this article. In fact, they just about suggest that trying to fix people is akin to witchcraft!"

Lucy laughed and said, "This people stuff is all witchcraft as far as I can see. All these classes on personal improvement spin a lot of wheels, but the same people come back to the same jobs, and I don't see much difference." Pete said that from his experience he had to agree.

Kip nodded his head in agreement, too, and said, "Let me add some fuel to that fire. Remember, these researchers are stating that it isn't about fixing people or offering them incentives. Instead, they found that it's about changing the context, or philosophy, of the workplace."

Kip read from the article, "'Change in attitudes or personal improvement, the [old] theory goes, leads to changes in individual behavior.' The three professors go on to say that that approach gets the change process exactly backward. Their research reveals that, as they put it, 'individual behavior is powerfully shaped by the roles that people play' [whether it's a 'C' or 'F' environment].[1]

"The professors conclude that by first changing the environment—that is, by changing the roles people play and the responsibilities they assume—individual behavior changes and organizational results improve. Or, put another way, by creating an environment where people are encouraged to take responsibility, a foundation for accountability is established. They are really talking about changing from a control-based approach to a freedom-based one."

"But, you can't ask people to be accountable unless you give them choices and trust them," said Pete.

"And you're really talking about giving the people control of the context, meaning the systems and policies, aren't you?" asked Lucy.

Kip nodded, realizing that both Pete and Lucy were catching on fast.

Lucy added, "I agree that changing the environment or the context is the place to begin, if changing the environment means improving the processes. Personally, I don't see a problem with a top-down management approach that controls the processes. From my observations, most people aren't intrinsically motivated, as you put it, anyway," she said, turning toward Kip. "I believe it's well-defined and controlled processes that get people to be accountable," said Lucy in a punctuating tone.

"That's an interesting point of view, Lucy," commented Kip. "What makes you come to that conclusion?"

"Personal experience," responded Lucy.

"OK, I'll listen to your experience," responded Kip. "Convince me."

"Do you really want to hear my opinion?" asked Lucy in astonishment.

"Yes, I do," said Kip.

"OK, here goes. Some of the best management applications that I've been involved in introducing were TQM, ISO 9000, the Balanced Score Card, and now Six Sigma. All of these process programs can make a difference. I can tell you firsthand that each of these systems has improved the organizations I've worked with.

"To paraphrase W. Edwards Deming, the father of the quality movement, 'Fix the processes, not the people!'"

Pete saw Lucy as someone who knew her stuff and could go toe to toe with Kip.

"Deming was right on that point," conceded Kip. "You, of course, are familiar with Dr. Deming's famous marble exercise, right?"

"Of course," responded Lucy.

"What's this?" asked Pete, as he leaned forward to hear Kip's response.

Kip looked at Pete and began. "In the exercise, Dr. Deming has several members of the audience—preferably managers or Ph.D.s—come up to the podium and attempt to separate red from white marbles following a defined set of rules or, as you might guess, a process or system.

"Deming loved to have lots of fun with the Ph.D.s on stage, poking and prodding them on. I remember one time I saw Deming in Cleveland. He was great. You could see the folks sweating as they tried to perform the task Deming was demonstrating. Sorry for the digression, but I couldn't help it." Kip laughed and continued.

"The demonstration showed that it was not the individual's hard work, experience, or talent that affected the outcome of the sorting process but the game itself, or the system, that made the difference.

"So, here's my point. Deming stated that to achieve a different outcome you must fix the system and not the people— exactly what you said," he noted, looking at Lucy.

"Yes!" exclaimed Lucy. "Fix the system, not the people."

Kip, having made the first point to get Lucy on board, continued. "Yes, but many of Deming's disciples have taken the meaning of this demonstration too literally. They suggest that to achieve the desired outcome, we need only to craft the right processes and systems without considering people. But working with people isn't that simple.

"Processes play a major role for sure, but individual initiative, creativity, and personal choice play just as big a role or even bigger. That's what Sartre and deCharms were suggesting, and so was Deming.

"Lucy, it's not 'Fix the process and ignore the people.' People make the processes work. They always have and they always will."

Pete broke in. "Let me see if I understand what you're saying to us both. Yes, Deming said, 'Fix the process and not the people.' But your contention is that Deming was not completely heard.

"People focused on the processes to the exclusion of dealing with the people," continued Pete. "Reflecting out loud on this, it almost seems obvious that most of us would rather fix processes than wrestle people to the ground every day."

Kip nodded in agreement and took off from Pete's comments. "Pete, Deming's famous Fourteen Points outlines this very issue, if we're open to hearing what the man was really trying to tell us. Of his Fourteen Points, five suggest the need for a freedom-based environment. See if you agree: (1) 'Cease dependence on mass inspection'; (2) 'Drive out fear'; (3) 'Eliminate slogans, exhortations, and targets for the workforce'; (4) 'Eliminate numerical quotas'; and (5) 'Remove barriers to pride of workmanship.'"[2]

Kip continued. "Control-based executives, hungering for improved results, happily adopted Deming's models of statistical control, but they ignored his exhortations to treat people with dignity and respect. These business leaders meant well, but they were blind to the people side of the equation."

"Kip, maybe they weren't blind," interjected Pete. "Maybe they just didn't want to face up to the really hard stuff—the people stuff!"

Deming's Freedom-Based Points

1. *Cease dependence on mass inspection.*

2. *Drive out fear.*

3. *Eliminate slogans, exhortations, and targets for the workforce.*

4. *Eliminate numerical quotas.*

5. *Remove barriers to pride of workmanship.*

Lucy didn't want this to turn into a lovefest, so she challenged Pete's interpretation. "So, are you saying, Pete, that organizations that have invested in these programs are not getting their money's worth?"

Pete retorted, "Lucy, I'm a CEO, and I'm telling you from my experience that although we received some benefit from these programs, the ones you mentioned, we didn't get the long-term value we were promised. They didn't stick!"

He continued with a more passionate tone. "Kip's point is that processes alone won't cut it. People sustain processes because they want to. I remember going to a quality conference, where I sat next to a senior quality manager from one of America's largest aerospace organizations. Here's what he said: 'We aren't going to get quality at our organization until people want it. My department can't do it alone.'

"I've never forgotten his comment, and now it all makes sense. In the long run, without the enthusiastic support of our people, systems and policies alone won't get the job done. If they did, I could go on vacation more often with my family, and I wouldn't be going to L.A. right now," Pete smiled and then laughed.

"And after trying all these programs," he continued, "my people are more frustrated and fatigued than they were when we started down this road! But most critical of all is that we've run out of options!"

"What do you mean, you've run out of options?" asked Lucy, somewhat bewildered with Pete's seemingly throw-away line.

Pete chose his words carefully. He didn't want to be misunderstood by Lucy. "What I mean is that we've tried all the programs. This trip I'm on to L.A. is to smooth over relations with our partners because we can't deliver as promised using these programs. We've programmed our people to death. But they're not owners of these programs. These programs were imposed on them, and now I know it was wrong."

Kip could see the anger and frustration in Pete's face and expanded on Pete's point. "Lucy, it might seem a little radical, but I'm suggesting that the management programs you mentioned, as good as they are, will never sustain improvements in a control-based environment."

Management programs, as good as they are, will never sustain improvements in a control-based environment.

Lucy prided herself on her flexibility. Unlike Yolanda, who she concluded was defensive and rigid, she knew that she would not be overwhelmed by these men's opinions and that all programs or supposed solutions were never the total answer. She was a seeker of ideas—no, she was a goddess of ideas. She smiled, not taking herself too seriously. "OK," she said, "is there a compromise we can reach on this?"

"Yes," said Pete. "Your compromise solution, it seems, is this: I believe that if the processes we tried had been placed in a freedom-based work environment, they would have worked. Or, to say it another way, programs like the ones you mentioned won't be sustainable until we start trusting people

80

to make their own decisions. We have to move all our programs, policies, and systems over to an 'F' thinking operation.

"Additionally, top management can't and shouldn't decide on the processes or programs. We should leave it up to our people. We have no alternative but to trust them. And I believe that in many cases you wouldn't need the controls many processes offer if people were trusted and invited to be truly accountable." Kip smiled, knowing that Pete had just taken his ideas and made them his own.

Lucy was somewhat taken aback. She sat silently, looking Kip squarely in the eye like he had poisoned this CEO with his magic.

Kip looked back at Lucy with empathy and softened his voice. "Lucy, I have another story to tell you that happened several years ago when I attended an American Society of Training and Development (ASTD) conference at the Mascone Center in San Francisco.

"During that conference, an interesting conversation caught my attention. The idea that we can control people and not get caught up in the control-based context ourselves is an illusion. Also, we must realize that when we totally control a workplace with restrictions, fear, and heavy-handed methods, we pay an awful price in the long run.

"The story contrasts the difference between control and freedom and how it applies to a simple need, such as trying to get work done under the tyranny of controls, systems, and processes.

"A group of human resource employees from General Electric were swapping stories about life at GE under Jack Welch. Here is a man who was both feared and revered for his business acumen, a man who is the archetype of a control-based leader, and a guy who brought in process controls, top-grading appraisal systems, and management control measurements and took them to a new level.

"Well, several of his employees were talking about how his management system encouraged fear and waste rather than collaboration and efficiency. Imagine—fear and waste! They might not have used the freedom/control metaphor, but that's what they were talking about.

"One story in particular illustrated how CEO Jack Welch and his people had become victims of a top-down workplace. And the ironic thing is that Welch was trying to avoid waste, but his methods were, in many cases, draconian. The tragedy is that he never became aware of the detrimental effects fear had on the bottom line."

"So you're saying that as profitable as GE was, it could've been greatly improved?" asked Pete.

"That's what I am saying," answered Kip. "As the story was being told," he continued, "the group of people at the conference listened in shock, mostly because they had all read such wonderful financial reports about the organization and about Welch's publicly hailed leadership.

"One of the HR people began, saying, 'As I began my work experience at GE in upstate New York, I was assigned a desk in an open environment with forty-two-inch-high, movable walls. Sitting there was like sitting in the middle of a goldfish bowl.' Many of the listeners empathized, nodding in agreement and smiling," added Kip.

"'I had always had a regular office,' the man continued, 'you know, one where you could close the door when you needed to get something serious done? Well, not so in my new digs at GE.

"'After three days of distractions, I approached my supervisor requesting that I be allowed temporarily to do some of my work in one of the nearby darkened vacant offices. In fact, there were several offices near our work area that no one ever used, which seemed strange to me. But her reaction to my request was what was even stranger.

"'My supervisor's response was swift and emphatic: '*No one is allowed to use those offices!*'

"'I was stunned. The supervisor, leaning in toward my face, spoke softly, as though there were hidden microphones all around. "Please understand," she whispered with quivering fear, "we must keep those dark offices vacant. If Mr. Welch were to drop in on one of his unannounced inspections and see these offices in use, he might think we're overstaffed!" The supervisor went on whispering, "So, it's essential that we keep those offices vacant to demonstrate that we run a lean operation.'"

"Those of us who were listening to the story sat in silence; no one was smiling any longer," Kip concluded. "It was clear that everyone understood the full weight and implication of the story.

"Unfortunately, each of us had been a victim of a top-down environment at some time in our careers, and we'd all seen what this kind of corporate culture creates: actions born of jealousy, misunderstanding, hypocrisy, politics, game playing, waste, and fear."

Pete knew what this meant on a very personal basis. Kip's GE story really hit home. Lucy said nothing at this point. The trio sat at the table in silence.

7

Can We Overcome Human Nature by Trying to Control People?

Lucy stared out the window into the distance, no longer making eye contact with either Pete or Kip. After a few moments, she said, "Gentlemen, I thank you both for a great and interesting discussion. But I need to get some work done. I'm free for dinner, say, about five-thirty?"

Turning to Kip, she said, "Mr. Kiplinger, let's just say we agree to disagree at this point, shall we, but I do like your company. Mr. Williams, it was a pleasure meeting you." Lucy smiled and rose, walking through the dining car toward her compartment. As she passed the cigar-chomping Hank Striker, she glared at him with an air of disgust.

Lucy had been wrong about being invulnerable to a new idea. Kip's story had caused her to think some uncomfortable thoughts about her present philosophy and beliefs. GE was one of the organizations she had worked at in the Northeast, and she knew Kip wasn't far from the truth about Welch's personal impact.

She also knew that she would see Kip and Pete again that evening and wanted to be open to hear these new ideas. Finally, if they were right, she was prepared to jump ship and join a new navy—that much she knew about herself. She wasn't stuck on one idea or philosophy if it no longer made sense.

As the waiter cleared away the dishes, Pete said with candor, "I've met and worked with a lot of Lucys in my day, and I think she made some really good points. She's sharp! You know, I've thought for a while now that a top-down control system is the wrong solution in this day and age, but I never had a realistic alternative. Now, I think maybe there is one.

"I can buy into the idea that people are the most important part of the business mix and the one strategic advantage any company has. I just never knew how to unlock this treasure. Now I know that I'll never be able to unlock this treasure, the power and creativity of my people, as long as our operation practices control-based thinking. That much I can tell you, Kip."

Kip smiled and nodded in appreciation.

At that, Pete became more reflective and changed the subject. "I've been thinking about why we CEOs feel the need to control others and why it might be hard for people at every level, especially us old-timers, to feel comfortable in a freedom-based environment.

"Looking at this personally, I think our need to control comes from our fear of the unknown and our own limitations. It's this subconscious fear that drives us to seek control over others. We don't do it because we're evil or power-hungry. We do it because we feel out of control and know of no alternative to feeling safe."

I think our need to control comes from our fear of the unknown and our own limitations. It's this subconscious fear that drives us to seek control over others.

"Pete, I think you may be right," said Kip. "My theory is that fear is driven by our sense of vulnerability."

"I quite agree," said Pete. "Still, a lack of fear is a dangerous thing, too. Without an awareness of the real perils around us, our very lives might be at stake. Fear protects us from real danger. But, Kip, do you think we're born with fear? Or do we learn to fear? Is fear part of our human nature, or are we conditioned to fear?"

"I think human behavior is affected by both nature and nurture," responded Kip. "There's ample evidence to suggest that human nature is more hard-wired than we previously thought and that our environment is enormously influential."

Pulling another dog-eared folder from his briefcase, Kip opened it to the first page. "Listen to what Rabbi Harold S. Kushner has to say on the subject of human nature; I think you'll find his approach enlightening." He began reading:

> We human beings are such complicated creatures. We have so many needs, so many emotional hungers, and they often come into conflict with each other. . . . Our souls are split, part of us reaching for goodness, part of us chasing fame and fortune and doing questionable things along the way, as we realize that those two paths may diverge sharply. . . . Much of our lives, much of our energy will be devoted to closing that gap between the longings of our soul and the scoldings of our conscience, between our too-often conflicting needs for the assurance of knowing that we are good and the satisfaction of being told we are important.[1]

Pete realized that this was a heavier subject than he had given it credit, so he encouraged Kip to continue. "Please, go on."

"Human nature is a complicated subject and not one, I'm sure, we'll ever fully understand—certainly I never will," Kip observed. "But, as modern scientific researchers unravel the mysteries of our minds and bodies, there's mounting evidence that much of our behavior is indeed genetically determined.

"It seems our emotional tendencies and intellectual capacities are profoundly influenced by the genetic instructions passed on to us by our parents. Listen to what one researcher says on the subject." Kip turned to the next page in the folder and began reading: 'Genes can generate . . . shyness or a short temper as assuredly as they do long bones or a fair complexion.'[2] And how about this," he said, turning to the next page: "'There are control centers in our brains that determine our innate temperaments.'"[3]

Turning to another page, Kip said, "Two separate studies confirmed Darwin's theory of emotional expression. One says that people in every culture in every part of the world use the same facial expressions to express universally recognizable emotions.[4] The other concludes that because of the architecture of our brains, we all exhibit the same facial language when showing emotions like anger, affection, or fear.[5] They both came to essentially the same conclusion."

"My wife and I have traveled all over the world," interjected Pete, "and I must tell you that there has never been a country where the facial expressions are any different than the ones here."

Kip nodded. "Yep, that's what Darwin is saying. In my work with organizations all over the world, I've found that people share an equally predictable, perhaps genetic, response to their work environments. We all seem to be cut from the same cloth when it comes to our emotional response to both freedom and control."

"So are you saying that freedom-based environments could work anywhere in the world, whether it's in America, Germany, Thailand, Argentina, India, or Saudi Arabia?" asked Pete.

"Yes, Pete, that's exactly what I am saying," replied Kip. "In fact, I've personally helped organizations all over the world—in the United States, Europe, Africa, and Asia—install freedom-based environments with the same quantifiably positive results.[6]

"I believe people are people all over the globe, and to believe that we don't all love our country or our children is absolute nonsense. We may call our god different names, but spirituality is as common and normal a human need as is air, food, and water."

Pete thought for a moment and then concurred emphatically. "Kip, I agree!"

"Despite ample evidence of our capacity for selfishness, greed, and ambition," Kip asserted, "there is a great deal of data that show that the vast majority of human beings have a strong desire to behave ethically and compassionately."

Turning a page in his folder, Kip said, "Dr. Jerome Kagan, professor of psychology at Harvard University, writes, 'The desire to believe the self is ethically worthy . . . is universal.'[7] Rabbi Harold Kushner adds, 'We want—indeed we need—to think of ourselves as good people, though from time-to-time we find ourselves doing things that make us doubt our goodness.'[8]

"I've come to believe that it's the workplace environment," Kip went on, "that most influences the behavior of people within an organization. People not only *can* be trusted but *must* be trusted.

"Of course, society and organizations have the right and responsibility to protect the majority from the small minority who prove through their actions that they cannot give up dependence on control or they cannot be trusted."

"Kip, if you're right," proposed Pete, "then in a freedom-based environment, selfishness, greed, and envy would give way to selflessness, generosity, and joy in the success of others."

"Pete, I couldn't have said it better myself," Kip said, smiling. "As of yet, no control-based approach has unlocked the human spirit in the way that freedom-based approaches have. Personal freedom, free enterprise, entrepreneurship, self-expression, creativity, productivity, and long-term survival of organizations all seem to flourish when people are given choices. My firsthand experience tells me that freedom-based environments tend to bring out the best in everyone. And it seems that every control-based approach eventually falls on its face.

"Recently the ideas of human potential have become popular. This approach, I'm afraid, uses a more subtle form of control. The human potential theory operates on the assumption that people can be fixed, freed from fear, provided they are willing to be fixed. This theory argues that by focusing on personal weaknesses and by changing personal habits, the human predisposition to fear can be overcome and organizational change can be accomplished."

"So if I follow your reasoning, here's the flaw in the human potential approach," interjected Pete. "As individuals change their habits and address their weaknesses, as they become more self-assured and self-confident, they chafe at the continued attempts to fix them."

"Exactly, Pete. In fact, as people grow and get to know themselves, they increase their self-esteem and open the channels for more freedom, not more control."

Pete interrupted, "It's because they become freer and less fearful."

"Right!" exclaimed Kip. "And as individuals become accountable for their own choices and results, and as they become more self-confident in their ability to be great, they simply can no longer live in a management–employee context that continues to attempt to subtly manipulate or control them in a paternalistic way. And so, they eventually leave the organization looking for more freedom."

Pete broke in again with a sudden revelation. "That might account for the phenomenon of why so many women leave corporate life. Just look, for example, at the number of women who become successful entrepreneurs. They figure out early in their careers that the control-based ceilings and unspoken prejudices are not for them and choose to strike out on their own."

Kip, nodding in agreement, added, "A freedom-based organization takes a very different approach to organizational change and how it deals with the individual's unique talents. Paraphrasing Peter Drucker, the well-known author of a voluminous number of books and articles on management and organizational change, 'You don't improve organizational performance by focusing on personal or organizational weaknesses; you improve performance by capitalizing on strengths.'[9]

"It's by learning how to take advantage of our talents and strengths and by surrounding ourselves with others who possess gifts that complement our own," Kip added, "that we become successful together and are able to reject the need to use fear as a motivator."

"All right," said Pete, "I can see that we should reject fear as the primary means of motivating others and ourselves. But do you really think it's possible to eliminate fear completely from the workplace?"

You don't improve organizational performance by focusing on personal or organizational weaknesses; you improve performance by capitalizing on strengths.

"Of course not," said Kip. "But remember, Dr. Deming in his Fourteen Points on how to create a quality context exhorts us to drive fear out of the workplace!

"A freedom-based organization embraces the belief that creating an environment relatively free from fear—that is, free from reliance on control and manipulation— establishes accountability and sustains organizational results. And Deming goes on to say that it's management's responsibility to root out fear."

By now the dining car was empty except for the two men. Kip looked at his watch and said, "Pete, I need to make a call. I'll meet you back in the compartment. Let's let the staff clean up our table so they can take their break."

Pete nodded in agreement, and the two men left the dining car.

8

Three Activities That Establish a Freedom-Based Workplace

After his phone call, Kip returned to the cabin. Pete was catching a cat nap, and Kip let him rest. He had some reading to do, so he welcomed the time alone. He had pretty much finished what he wanted to do when Pete began to stir.

"I bet you needed that nap," said Kip with a grin.

"I sure did," Pete said, as he stretched his arms and legs. The nap had allowed his brain to crystallize and clarify many of the concepts Kip had set forth during their time together. Refreshed from his rest, Pete felt ready once again to tackle their earlier discourse. "Kip, I like the idea of a freedom-based organization, but I still have my doubts about whether it could work in my circumstances. For the sake of argument, how do you take the first step?"

"OK, Pete, for the sake of argument let me see if I can flesh out the approach I would suggest you take. I'll start by putting the approach in a perspective that creates long-term value, one that sustains organizational results and gets people to be accountable."

And so Kip began. "What is needed, what is absolutely essential, is one decision and three activities. The decision you need to make first is that this is the journey you want to take. Next, you need to begin these activities in parallel," and he wrote three activities on a yellow pad of paper:

1. **Grant individual freedom as a right:** Give people the freedom to make choices.

2. **Ask everyone to take personal responsibility:** Allow people to design and own their jobs and create their own systems.

3. **Have faith in people:** Believe that everyone wants to be great, and trust them to do great things.

Kip handed the paper to Pete, saying, "These are the cornerstones of the freedom-based approach and philosophy. Let me start with some background on the first activity."

Kip circled his first notation—"Grant individual freedom as a right: Give people the freedom to make choices"—with his pen. "First, you've got to create an environment that gives people the individual freedom to experiment and explore new ideas. This means giving people choices and control over their own jobs, and it means that you must let go of the idea that there is only one way of doing a task."

Pete interrupted. "That idea alone would drive Lucy up a wall, wouldn't it?"

"Yes, I'm afraid it would," affirmed Kip, matching Pete's grin. "Most important, being given individual freedom means being treated with respect and dignity by everyone in the organization. Titles and status have very little meaning. It comes down to the content of the person's idea, not who's saying it."

"That sounds mighty close to a speech that Dr. Martin Luther King delivered on the steps of the Washington Monument," related Pete. "I was there. It was a thrilling experience. I took off from grad school to drive down with a group of friends. It's one of my most prized memories."

Kip smiled in acknowledgment, remembering the early days of the civil rights movement when a group of Americans began fighting together for their God-given right to be first-class citizens.

"Giving people individual freedom is a scary thought! This is a tough one," Pete sighed in resignation.

Kip looked deeply into Pete's eyes. "Pete, if you're not committed to giving people individual freedom, don't even attempt this. Making the leap to a freedom-based philosophy takes guts and genuine commitment on the part of leadership. Embracing this approach and philosophy represents a radical departure from the well-worn paths of control-based applications. Like a sailor boarding a small sailboat, you can't place one foot in the freedom boat while leaving the other foot on the control dock. Doing so places you in jeopardy of falling into the water."

"This is beginning to sound like a speech," said Pete with a wink.

"Actually, it is a speech of sorts. Over the years I've worked with many CEOs who have asked, 'Where do I start?' And this is where you start!" said Kip.

"Creating a freedom-based organization takes time, at least three to four years to make the change," he continued. "For many organizations, it takes much longer. It took Johnsonville Foods a decade or more to get there because they lacked a road map. We now have lots of road maps, but most are more similar than dissimilar.

"It's tough to break away from a dependence on control-based management systems that take away individual freedoms for the purpose of meeting goals and making the numbers."

Pete broke in. "With our quarter-to-quarter focus, we rarely look further ahead than a year or two at a time. And we've abandoned a lot of programs that have failed to produce results in less time."

"Pete, in all likelihood," said Kip, "not all of those programs you abandoned were flawed—just like I told Lucy. Many management programs fail because the work environment doesn't give people the individual freedom they need to make them work. And, unfortunately, organizations don't stay with these programs long enough to see the fruits of their efforts. They get impatient, and that's the kiss of death."

"But, Kip, even when I've given my people more individual freedom, a lot of them seem unwilling to accept that much responsibility."

"That brings me to my second point," Kip said as he picked up his pen again and circled his second activity—"'Ask everyone to take personal responsibility: Allow people to design and own their jobs and create their own systems.' People must be given the personal responsibility of owning their job and being accountable for their results. In fact, you must insist upon it!

"When you really look closely at control-based systems, people at the bottom are never accountable; their bosses are. That's why incentives are used to motivate people who don't own anything! After all, since the boss sets the goals and monitors the results, he or she is the only one who's really committed to them.

"On the other hand, if you want people at every level to be accountable, they've got to set their own goals and monitor their own results."

Pete interrupted and said, "Excuse me, but I think you're touching on an important point. What you're saying is that people are never going to be responsible unless they own their job, and to own their job they need a stake in the outcome."

"Pete, that's exactly right. The guy who owns the ball makes the rules. And everyone else is just a player—not an owner," said Kip in summary. "Once your people accept personal responsibility for making their own choices, they become accountable for their results. Regardless of the workplace environment, the person who sets the goal is always the accountable party."

"But," countered Pete, "do you honestly believe every staff member is capable of being personally responsible for making his or her own choices and of being accountable?"

"Let me ask you a question, Pete," countered Kip. "Do you honestly believe there is a single person on your staff who, when hired, didn't intend to do his or her very best? And if that person did, the real question is, 'What happened to him or her?'"

"That's what I've been wondering for years, Kip," said Pete, with obvious frustration in his voice, "and that's why I'm on this train in the first place when I could be with my family putting up our Christmas tree!"

You can't expect people to take risks if you continue to insist that they seek approval for every action! You can't craft policies and procedures based on the assumption that people can't be trusted, while at the same time expecting them to use their best judgment and to do the right thing! And you can't dictate policies and at the same time empower people. It just won't work!

"Think about it, Pete." Kip kept hitting Pete hard. "You can't restrict the flow of information and then wonder why nobody knows what's going on! You can't expect people to take risks if you continue to insist that they seek approval for every action! You can't craft policies and procedures based on the assumption that people can't be trusted, while at the same time expecting them to use their best judgment and to do the right thing!

"And—you can't dictate policies and at the same time empower people. It just won't work!"

Pete thought for a long while before he finally said, "I'm not sure I've got the right people to make a freedom-based environment work. They've just disappointed me too often."

Kip understood all too well Pete's concern. "This leads us to the third and last activity you need to do to get started," said Kip as he circled the third activity—"'Have faith in people: Believe that everyone wants to be great and trust them to do great things.'

"You must have a fundamental faith in people," resumed Kip. "As I said before, you've got to hire people you can trust and then trust them completely. Making a freedom-based environment work requires that you stop managing people and stop trying to control them.

"The two philosophies of control and freedom cannot coexist. That's a fundamental truth!" he emphasized. "People will sometimes disappoint you. But when they do, it's your moment of truth that will challenge your commitment to the freedom-based philosophy. Do you hold the course, or do you go back to a control-based approach? And if you think you have problems in this area, just check out the Book of Job in the Bible for inspiration," said Kip with a wink.

The two philosophies of control and freedom cannot coexist. That's a fundamental truth!

"Now that's a leap of faith," said Pete, shaking his head and smiling. Then he turned to Kip in serious concern and said, "I'm not sure I want to abandon the systems we've put in place. After all, managing people is the only way we've been able to get them to be halfway accountable."

"My definition of a manager," said Kip with a smile, "is someone who has done such a poor job of hiring that he or she has now got to watch the poor devils on a full-time basis."

A look of mild amusement passed across Pete's face.

"Pete, it's simply not possible to get people to be accountable using control-based systems, and the evidence is clear on this point," said Kip. "You've got to make a choice between controls and freedom to achieve accountability. No amount of incentives, systems, policies, or personal improvement training will get you to the point of enjoying accountability at every level of your operation. It just won't happen."

A manager is someone who has done such a poor job of hiring that he or she has now got to watch the poor devils on a full-time basis.

Pete didn't respond immediately. He stared out the window at the countryside blanketed with snow, then turned to Kip and said, "I still don't think you've answered my question, so I'll ask it in a different way. Isn't it possible that I've got people in my organization that need to be managed, people I must control?"

Kip answered carefully to make sure that Pete got the message. "Pete, in my experience only about 5 percent of your people fall into that category. And for that small percentage, you'll ultimately come to the conclusion that they simply cannot stay. As harsh as it sounds, that's the truth. But why build your system based on the 5 percent? I believe you need to build your system on the 95 percent."

As Pete reflected on Kip's last statement, he decided that now seemed a good time to go back to something he had observed on his way back to their compartment after lunch. "Kip, I want to change the subject a little," Pete began, "but maybe it's really on the same subject. As I was coming back to the compartment after lunch, I couldn't help but overhear the loud guy with the cigar.

"Our friend Hank Striker is in a compartment near ours, and I heard him unloading his views on a captive traveler seated next to him. I almost burst out laughing when I saw who was with him. You guessed it—our dining room companion Yolanda. He was telling her that he had nothing but lazy morons working for him. He went on to say that if he wasn't watching them every moment, nothing would get done! His unwilling companion stared into her lap and tried not to make eye contact."

"So what's the question?" asked Kip.

"Well, the question is, what am I going to do with all the Hank Strikers in my organization? I've got a few older union guys and supervisors who don't know any way other than to bully people. They may have good hearts, but they're part of my existing problem, and they also put out a lot of work."

"OK, let me first answer your question," responded Kip. "First of all, some people will just not stay when you start dishing out freedom. Pete, it's going to take an extremely different approach in working with people. That's a lesson I learned early in my journey.

"Now to your second point, about the guy with Yolanda. As you were overhearing that guy, did it hit you that maybe under your breath you'd made some very similar statements at one time or another? I must admit, until I saw the light, I said the same things about my staff! I hate to confess, but I wasn't too far off of our friend Striker myself on occasions. Maybe I didn't shout at people, but I got close.

"But, Pete, don't be too hard on him or yourself. Every CEO in a control-based operation feels the same way as that man does from time to time. I can see some of myself in him because I frequently blamed my people in the old days. But after my wake-up call, I would catch myself, take responsibility for my mistake, and ask for forgiveness."

Kip was ready to move on to another subject. "Is it OK if we change the subject?"

"Sure," said Pete smiling. "I'm satisfied with your answer to my question."

At that point, Kip pulled out a tattered paperback from his briefcase entitled *The Art of Japanese Management*. He held up the book in front of Pete and said, "This is the book that first got me thinking about freedom-based work environments, before I made that call to my operations VP Jennifer.

"The book was written in 1981 by Harvard and Stanford professors Richard Pascale and Anthony Athos. They highlight the contrast in corporate culture between the Japanese powerhouse Matsushita Electric (Panasonic) and the American organization ITT. ITT in 1979 was the fifth largest employer in America, with revenues of over $22 billion.

"At the time, Harold Geneen, CEO of ITT, was the darling of corporate America. His methods were even taught in business schools.

"But shortly after he left ITT in 1979, the heavily debt-laden conglomerate began a seven-year slide into oblivion. Pascale and Athos's book describes a control-based management system at ITT that even included an internal spy network. In contrast, Matsushita Electric was run on a philosophy of accountability, honor, and trust."

"But ITT's story isn't necessarily representative of what happens in control-based operations," argued Pete. "I see accounts of successful control-based operations in the financial pages of business newspapers and magazines every week, and they've been successful for years."

"We're all looking for 'success formulas' to emulate," said Kip. "And the media is glad to oblige us with articles and books about organizations that have achieved extraordinary financial performance.

"I've noticed over the years, however, that most of the companies held up as models of success are unable to sustain their success for the long term. Just look at the number of companies that have faltered since the book *In Search of Excellence* was written. Almost every company cited as an excellent organization has fallen on hard times."

"And now I think I know why!" responded Pete. "But can you give me an example of a CEO who made the leap to a freedom-based environment and saw it pay off?"

"Sure," answered Kip. "Here's an article that appeared in the April '96 issue of *Fast Company*." Kip handed the article to Pete. "Look at what Mort Meyerson had to say about his experience at EDS."

Pete begins to read aloud:

In purely financial terms, my seven years running EDS had been unbelievably successful. When I left, I was proud of the people, the company, and our achievements. From the day I started as president in 1979 to the day I left in 1986, EDS never had a single quarter where we lost money. We never even had a quarter where we were flat—every quarter we grew like gangbusters. That kind of economic performance made a lot of our people very rich. I used to take enormous pride in the fact that I was instrumental in getting a lot of equity into the hands of the people at EDS.[1]

Pete stopped reading and blurted out, "Most CEOs would kill to get those kind of results!"

"True enough," agreed Kip. "But wait until you read what Meyerson says next."

Pete read further:

> What I realized after I left was that I had also made a lot of people very unhappy. Our people paid a high price for their economic success. . . . The system worked; that is, we got exactly what we wanted. We asked people to put financial performance before everything else, and they did. They drove themselves to do whatever was necessary to create those results—even if it meant too much personal sacrifice or doing things that weren't really in the best interests of customers. Sometimes they did things that produced positive financial results in the short term but weren't in the company's long-term interest. . . . The emphasis on profit-and-loss to the exclusion of other values was creating a culture of destructive contention.[2]

"When Ross Perot recruited Meyerson to be the CEO of Perot Systems in 1992, Meyerson spent six months visiting with Perot Systems associates and customers. Then he met with Ross and reported, 'Everything I thought I knew about leadership is wrong.'"

"Meaning what?" questioned Pete.

"Meaning that everything had changed, including the technology, the customers, the market, and what people in the organization expected from the organization."

"So what did Meyerson do?" questioned Pete.

"Put simply, he made the decision to implement a freedom-based environment at Perot Systems," answered Kip. "Meyerson realized he needed to be a different kind of leader this time around."

"And how's it worked out, Kip?" asked Pete.

"It's worked out very well," Kip responded. "Not only is Perot Systems now more people-friendly; the results can be seen on their P&L and balance sheet.

"Pete, when I read Pascale and Athos's account of the ITT corporate culture and Meyerson's description of life at EDS,

I was struck by the similarity of those cultures to our own at National Stores," revealed Kip.

"So these two stories helped convince you that a leap to a freedom-based environment was worth the risk?" asked Pete.

"These and many others," confirmed Kip. "I felt like I was looking into a mirror when I read these stories. And I started to understand why my people weren't accountable. It was because of me! When I began to believe in my people and demonstrated that faith with my actions and reactions, things started to change. My people started showing the light of greatness that we thought we'd seen when we hired them.

"Let me quote David Kessler and the late Elisabeth Kubler-Ross, who wrote eloquently about this: 'Everyone carries the seeds of greatness. "Great" people don't have something that everyone else doesn't; they've simply removed a lot of the things that stand in the way of their best selves.'[3]

Everyone carries the seeds of greatness. "Great" people don't have something that everyone else doesn't; they've simply removed a lot of the things that stand in the way of their best selves.

"I was the biggest thing that stood in the way of my people's best selves," admitted Kip. "Because I had no faith in them, they felt no loyalty to me or to the company. It's the leader that everyone ultimately looks to for inspiration. If the right signals aren't there, the people will read the signs. You just can't fake it!

"So as I began to understand, accept, and apply the principles of a freedom-based environment, faith in people, and personal accountability, people's loyalty improved and they began doing great things.

"Speaking of loyalty, I've got a copy of an article I read recently in the MIT *Sloan Management Review* about the relationship between ethics and loyalty. And that's another basic lesson anyone who wants people to be accountable needs to learn: Integrity is a key ingredient in creating a freedom-based workplace."

Kip passed the article to Pete and started to explain it. "Katherine J. Sweetman cites a global study of the effects of organizational ethics on employee loyalty. Two leading research groups conducted the study: Walker Information Global Network and the Hudson Institute. They surveyed more than 9,700 employees from business, nonprofit, and government organizations in thirty-two countries around the globe. Although this article focuses on ethics and loyalty, it's really another lesson in accountability. Listen to what the research showed.

"Fully one half of employees worldwide, according to the survey, felt their companies were not ethical, and therefore they felt very little loyalty to their companies. These same employees, Sweetman points out, tended to become highly unproductive and highly likely to abandon the organization at the earliest opportunity." Kip added, "These are descriptions of nonaccountable behavior."

Pete interjected, "That makes sense, Kip, but isn't it possible for a control-based environment to be ethical?"

"Of course it is, and most are, to my knowledge," responded Kip. "But people don't really separate ethics from how they are treated on a daily basis, and that's the lesson I learned from Sweetman. If they feel miserable on the job, they very naturally conclude that they're not being treated ethically. Now you may want to fight me on this, but the data support my view and experience.

"On the other hand, those employees who felt their companies were highly ethical showed high levels of loyalty and exhibited the very behaviors that make organizations successful: 'working hard, staying late, going the extra mile for customers, and recommending their company to their friends as a good place to work.'[4] Pete, isn't this another way of describing accountable behavior?"

"I'd love to see more of that kind of accountability at my company!" exclaimed Pete.

"Then the question is obvious," Kip said. "How does an organization create the conditions where the employees show loyalty and do great things?"

Pete answered, "This last piece of evidence you've shown me suggests that if you want a truly loyal group of employees, you need to treat them ethically, *and* you need to treat them the way you'd want to be treated—with dignity, respect, and trust."

"That's what I've concluded," said Kip.

The younger man interjected: "Kip, maybe you've put your finger on the reason we've been losing some of our best young people recently, especially our top women. Maybe what we've identified as a lack of loyalty in the younger generation is really a reflection of the way we've been treating them.

"In exit interviews, we've had complaints, especially from the women, on what drives them crazy. These younger people feel constrained by all the controls that don't seem to bother our older workers. But we can't afford to lose anyone, especially not our future generation of leaders."

CREATING

the

TRANSFORMATION

9

The Transformation of National Stores: A Journey from the Old Control-Based Environment to the New Freedom-Based Workplace

The steward knocked softly on the door as he slid it open. "Gentlemen, dinner will be served beginning at four-thirty. I just wanted to let you know now so that you can plan accordingly."

"Thank you very much," replied Pete. "We'd like to reserve a table for three of us."

Pete turned to Kip and said, "Remember, Lucy wants to join us." Kip nodded. "Could you stop by at around five-fifteen, and let us know if there are any tables available, and also let Ms. Lucy Woo know? I don't know what compartment she's in," said Pete.

Kip turned to Pete. "Considering the circumstances, why don't we bail Yolanda out of her predicament with our buddy Hank Striker?"

"Not a bad idea," said Pete smiling. "Who knows, if we're lucky, Striker might join us." The two men laughed, and Kip signaled with his hands that that was a mischievous idea.

"I'd be happy to reserve a table for you gentlemen and to inform the ladies of your invitation. What is the other woman's last name so we might look it up?" said the steward.

Pete replied, "Her name is Yolanda Worthington."

As the steward continued down the corridor, Pete said, "Kip, have you noticed how good the service has been on this train?"

"You're right, Pete. The whole staff is just great—the conductor, the steward, the waiters, the porters, everyone. It's one of the reasons I travel by train between Chicago and L.A. Even though it takes longer than flying, the service on this route is always superior, and I'm willing to take the added time."

"I wish I got this kind of service everywhere I went," ruminated Pete.

"You would if more people understood the power of a freedom-based work environment," observed Kip. "When people, like the staff on this train, accept responsibility for delivering great service, it's the customers who benefit. After all, as we discovered at National Stores, our ultimate accountability is always to our customers."

"Say, I've been meaning to ask you," said Pete, "how'd your organization make the transformation?"

"We took it one step at a time, and it wasn't easy," replied Kip. "We had a lot of 'people from Missouri'—you know, people who need to be convinced."

Kip reflected a moment and then began: "When National Stores started the journey toward a freedom-based organization, we thought that in order to be personally accountable to others, we needed to give up individual freedom for the good of the organization.

"But we quickly learned that individual members needed the individual freedom to choose the work best suited to their talents, skills, and interests if the organization was going to benefit. Creating a healthy organization required a willingness on our part to include people who perhaps didn't initially share our views.

"Healthy organizations," emphasized Kip, "embody a spirit of inclusion by offering hospitality to everyone. *Hospitality* is an old-fashioned word that means 'a generous and cordial reception.'[1]

. "Of course, offering hospitality was easy when those we included were like us. But the real test came when we faced the challenge of offering hospitality to those who were unlike us, to those who didn't share our views or our cultural norms.

Healthy organizations embody a spirit of inclusion by offering hospitality to everyone. Hospitality *is an old-fashioned word that means "a generous and cordial reception."*

"Yet by extending hospitality to everyone at National Stores, we broke down the walls of insecurity that separated us. Extending hospitality had a wonderfully therapeutic effect for both the recipients and the givers, and the customers felt the difference."

"What do you mean, therapeutic?" asked Pete.

"As Kathleen Norris puts it in her book *Amazing Grace,* 'hospitality has a way of breaking through the defenses of insularity [insulating oneself from others],'"[2] explained Kip. "By creating an inclusive and hospitable organization at National Stores, we created healthy relationships free from the fear-induced need to control others and to protect ourselves from new ideas that we had previously found threatening. Being inclusive and offering hospitality proved to be therapeutic for us.

"When we were living under a control-based environment, on the other hand, we couldn't tolerate contamination from people outside the management group. We became exclusive, repelling new ideas and repelling people whose ideas didn't conform to our own. We were cutting ourselves off from our own future.

"Recently I came across an article in the *Christian Science Monitor.* What caught my attention was a graphic that summarizes this very point about the contrast between *resistant* and *progressive* cultures." At that, Kip pulled the graphic from his briefcase.

ACCOUNTABILITY

How Organizations Get People to Be Accountable

FACTOR	PROGRESS-PRONE CULTURE	PROGRESS-RESISTANT CULTURE
Time orientation	Future	Present or past
Mind set	I can influence my destiny.	Fatalism, resignation
Competition	Leads to excellence	Aggression
Advancement	Merit	Family, connections
Justice, fair play	A reality	A myth
Authority	Dispersed: checks, balances (Rule of law)	Centralized: unfettered (rule of man)
Church/state	Secularized	Religion plays major role in civic sphere.
Work achievement	Live to work: Wealth is good.	Work to live: Poverty is good.

SOURCE: *Christian Science Monitor*

"The article was comparing third world countries to modern societies," explained Kip. "But what struck me was that the article defining resistant cultures closely mirrored our old control-based behaviors at National Stores!"

"So this article isn't about American workplaces, is it?" remarked Pete.

"No, Pete," said Kip. "The article was about third world countries, which, at the risk of generalizing for a moment, tend to be nondemocratic and in many cases repressive and corrupt."

"So," interjected Pete, "what you are saying is that whether it is a political or economic entity, freedom-based operations are progressive and open to new thinking and ideas, while repressive control-based regimes are threatened by new ideas and inclusion."

"And the net financial results," added Pete, "are staggering, because most of the repressive governments around the world are also wallowing in poverty."

"Yes," said Kip, "that's exactly what I thought as I read this article." He stopped for a moment to let what he had just said sink in. Then he continued.

"In fact, at National Stores I noticed, in retrospect, that we had displayed some of the same characteristics common to cults. We appeared elitist and exclusive, relying on strong, charismatic leaders using authoritarian power structures. We tended to regulate the flow of information. We developed an information-as-needed policy. We attempted to control employee behavior with personal improvement seminars, discouraged employees from critical thinking, and expected only managers to make decisions. We isolated and labeled as troublemakers people who failed to conform to our thinking. We totally stifled the free exchange of new ideas. We became rigid without knowing why."

"To be honest with you, Kip, that description sounds uncomfortably like our organization," observed Pete.

"I'm not surprised, Pete. Most organizations I encounter seem to suffer from the same symptoms. While these behaviors created group cohesiveness in the management team, they didn't contribute to a healthy and inclusive community. Authoritarian controls worked only as long as employees remained willing to comply with our orders and view of the world. The younger folks, I'm afraid, were discouraged and driven off by these practices.

"Under my old leadership, our management team used controls in an attempt to motivate employees to conform. In actuality, we fractured our relationships with the very people on whom we depended most! We eventually realized our mistake and sought to create a healthy and inclusive community. And to do so, we needed to invite our people to join with us, not work for us. This allowed us all to support one another as we implemented change."

Pete just shook his head in recognition that what Kip was talking about as the history of National Stores mirrored the current culture at his operation.

The older man continued: "In the old days, when we tried to impose change using control-based methods, the change we imposed from the top was nearly always met with resistance from those who felt victimized and excluded. In fact, because we'd introduced so many change and improvement programs in the past without sticking with them, we faced a crisis of credibility about as large as Richard Nixon had in his final months in office."

"I know exactly what you're saying, Kip," broke in Pete. "Our management team's credibility has suffered for the same reasons. And that's one of the things I'm most afraid of. Why should our people even believe me? I've let them down so often in the past."

Kip smiled, nodding knowingly. "Workers at National Stores learned from experience that most change programs would be abandoned after a period of time because more important issues would surface, diverting precious time and resources away from the new program. For those programs that stuck around longer than others, mere apathy was sufficient to kill them. The prevailing strategy employed by workers was 'If you wait long enough, this program, too, will eventually fade away.' It was a great stalling tactic, and it usually worked!"

The prevailing strategy employed by workers was "If you wait long enough, this program, too, will eventually fade away."

"Once again, you're describing our organization to a tee," added Pete sadly.

Kip nodded. "We eventually changed our approach and included our people in making changes."

"A good example of an organization that built their business on inclusion and hospitality is Nordstrom department stores. Established in 1900, Nordstrom is *the* name synonymous with customer service. They did it by creating a freedom-based culture. Nordstrom became famous for their policy of allowing sales people to exchange any and all customer returns with no questions asked."

"How did they pull it off without losing their shirt?" asked Pete.

"They did it by asking their people to follow one simple rule: 'Use your good judgment in all situations.'[3] Let me show you their unique five-by-seven-inch, one-page employee handbook[4]:

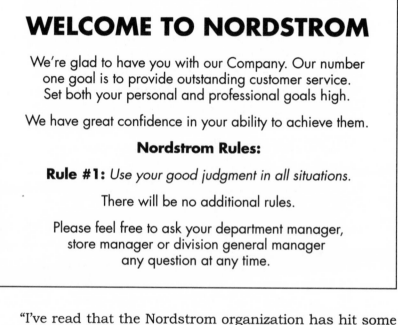

WELCOME TO NORDSTROM

We're glad to have you with our Company. Our number
one goal is to provide outstanding customer service.
Set both your personal and professional goals high.

We have great confidence in your ability to achieve them.

Nordstrom Rules:

Rule #1: *Use your good judgment in all situations.*

There will be no additional rules.

Please feel free to ask your department manager,
store manager or division general manager
any question at any time.

"I've read that the Nordstrom organization has hit some bumps in recent years," remarked Pete. "According to some business pundits, their continued success is somewhat in question. In fact, I saw an article that said they had forfeited their number one position in dollars sold per square foot, the gold standard of retail sales. Like so many organizations before them, Nordstrom seems to have lost their way."

"Yes," replied Kip, "but now the Nordstrom family is reorienting the basic core focus back squarely onto their original business values of trusting their people and letting them make the tough decisions. Of course, only time will tell whether they'll find their way back to their past successful formula. Thank goodness we found our way at National Stores!"

"There's got to be more to the transformation than just a healthy and inclusive community, isn't there?" asked Pete.

"Of course there is. Developing a willingness to experiment with ideas even when we initially disagreed was our next big challenge," said Kip. "It was one of the keys to getting people to become personally responsible for making choices. Our people needed to develop the competence to experiment with new ideas that were not yet completely understood.

"When you think about it, the natural curiosity of preschool children is, in part, motivated by their need to feel competent in dealing with their world. Workers at National Stores developed this important competency. They learned to take on what are called 'optimal challenges.'[5]

> ## *Developing a willingness to experiment with ideas even when we initially disagreed was our next big challenge.*

"A willingness to experiment depends on one's ability to create optimal challenges, and an optimal challenge is one that is neither ridiculously easy nor impossibly difficult. Optimal challenges, while difficult, are perceived by those pursuing them as being within the realm of possibility. When you ask people to become personally responsible for choosing their own optimal challenges, they become intrinsically motivated to give their best effort. They are more willing to experiment with new ideas, even when they don't fully understand them."

"Kip, wasn't it pretty hard to get people to be willing to take chances and experiment?" asked Pete.

"You're right on that point," confirmed Kip. "It's darn tough! At first folks thought it was a trick or something, but over time we won the battle, and now you can't stop people at every level from trying new ideas all the time. The only caveat we ask is that people keep us informed," said Kip with some pride.

"World-class athletes understand the concept of optimal challenge very well," he continued. "They learn how to tap into their own intrinsic motivation by setting goals that they can picture but that are just beyond their reach. We learned at National Stores that by tapping the power of optimal challenge, we could create a new willingness to experiment."

"Optimal challenge sounds a bit theoretical, Kip," Pete interjected. "Wouldn't it be simpler to offer a bonus for coming up with new ideas that work?"

"Now you're starting to sound like Yolanda," retorted Kip, smiling. "Perhaps I am getting a little theoretical, but the studies I showed you earlier indicate that the strategy of offering rewards to encourage experimentation actually damages people's motivation to pursue optimal challenges and to experiment.

"It didn't take us long to discover that by offering money, we, too, had damaged the willingness of our people to experiment and take risks. Remember, we all had bought into the behaviorist paradigm, including me. It wasn't easy to change our thinking, but we finally did!"

"So if you no longer put your faith in money to motivate, what did you put your faith in?" asked Pete.

"We put our faith in people! Believing in people gave our people choices, or what Dr. Nathaniel Branden calls 'true autonomy' in his book *Taking Responsibility*. Dr. Branden's studies, as well as the work of Dr. Edward Deci and other researchers, show very interesting results. By simply giving people choices of what tasks to undertake and how to do them, people are more engaged by the tasks and enjoy them more than those who are given no choices. Individuals who develop a healthy sense of autonomy are able to make wise choices, which enables them to take responsibility and to be accountable.[6]

"Dr. Branden describes autonomy this way." Holding a paper he pulled from his folder, Kip began reading:

Autonomy pertains to self-regulation: Control and direction from within, rather than from any external-authority. Autonomy is expressed through an individual's capacity for independent survival supporting and maintaining one's existence through productive work, independent thinking looking at the world through one's own eyes, and independent judgment honoring inner signals and values.[7]

"At National Stores," continued Kip, "we learned that when people were engaged in making their own decisions and in recognizing their limits and the limitations, their willingness to take personal responsibility and to become accountable increased, while their sense of alienation decreased.

"By providing people with choices, we arrived at better, more workable solutions.[8] By giving people choices at National Stores, within the apparent limits, people were more apt to give their best because it gave them a sense of control and autonomy."

"Excuse me for interrupting, Kip, but how do you ensure that high standards are established and met?"

"We didn't ignore standards by giving people choices, nor did we advocate permissiveness," explained Kip. "The challenge for us as leaders was to both support an individual's right to choose and yet help make the limits and responsibilities a person owned clear. This was accomplished not by ruling over people but by teaching and mentoring.

"Of course, as you pointed out earlier, Pete, reality often dictated that leaders had to be involved in setting limits. This meant that our leadership needed to learn to take the staff's perspective, to see the limits and choices from the employee's point of view. The person being limited had to be involved in understanding and setting the limits, so he or she didn't feel controlled or manipulated by them.[9] By taking this approach, we ensured that the standards were met.

"For example, I might say, 'I know it would be fun to do this task any way you'd like each time, but other people in the organization need to be able to count on the consistency of your work in order to complete their own tasks. Now, what do you think would be the best way to get this done every time?' Allowing each of our staff to choose his or her own best way satisfied each person's need for autonomy while, at the same time, everyone understood that limits are inherent in completing any task."

"That seems like a very practical approach, and I think it might even get Lucy's approval," said Pete smiling.

"Identifying limits without imposing controls is more easily said than done, however," retorted Kip. "Setting limits in an autonomy-supportive[10] fashion requires a great deal more effort and skill than applying our old, familiar coercive strategies.

"Interpersonal skills have an enormous impact on how limits are perceived; the words we choose make a big difference. The fewer controlling words we use, like *should* and *have to,* the better people perform."

"So that's how your leaders speak to your employees?" said Pete.

"Well, most of the time," conceded Kip. "Not controlling required a deep honesty that eluded many of us initially. For example, some of us insisted that we were encouraging employees by praising their good choices and constructively criticizing their poor ones. It later became painfully obvious to us that this strategy was a thinly veiled attempt to manipulate and that constructive criticism ultimately had a negative tinge to it.

It later became painfully obvious to us that this strategy was a thinly veiled attempt to manipulate and that constructive criticism ultimately had a negative tinge to it.

"So in order to put your faith in people," Pete summed up, "you had to give your people choices."

"You've got it!" said Kip enthusiastically. "And that's the concept that Yolanda needs to embrace."

Pete knew that Kip spoke with a deep understanding of how seductive incentives are.

10

The Wise Counsel

"**K**ip, you seem to be describing a leader who's different from the traditional leadership models I grew up with," observed Pete.

"Quite true," agreed Kip. He grabbed his yellow pad and wrote concepts 1, 2, and 3 while he spoke.

"Freedom-based leadership employs three primary strategies: (1) mentoring people by sharing a Keen Internal Vision, (2) becoming a resource to your people, and (3) waiting to be asked—don't take responsibility for the staff's activities and commitments. We call this kind of leader a Wise Counsel."[1] At that Kip showed Pete a printed sheet he had compiled about the role of the Wise Counsel.

"As a longtime control-based manager, the very thought of waiting to be asked strikes fear in my heart," said Pete.

"Pete, it would," said Kip, "because control-based management systems expect people to do what they're told without asking questions. In a control-based work environment, waiting to be asked, more often than not, would be disastrous."

Pete interjected, "Yeah, it's in the supervisors' job descriptions to be proactive in their leadership, not to wait."

The Two Major Roles of the Wise Counsel

Role 1: Create the Context for Accountability

- *Creates the conditions for responsibility-taking*

- *Gives the team time to own their tasks and share leadership*

- *Gets others to fully commit to the task through influence, not mandate*

- *Helps teams and individuals get to know each other—connects people to people*

- *Helps teams or individuals cooperatively work together*

- *Reinforces ground rules and reminds others of their responsibilities and right to choose*

- *Encourages participation from every member, but doesn't intimidate nor manipulate*

- *Works out decision-making issues through good strategic thinking, but never assumes responsibility for the decision or persuades others to one point of view*

- *Encourages responsibility-taking behavior, but doesn't delegate tasks*

- *Encourages shared leadership and discourages anyone from becoming the new control-based leader*

- *Provides ongoing feedback to the group on their progress as it relates to process, issues, and timing*

- *Attends meetings and helps create an atmosphere of collegial openness, mutual respect, and creative risk taking*

- *Encourages groups to follow a decision-making model based on gathering information first, then identifying the problem, task, or issue, in that order*

Role 2: Mentor without Taking Responsibility

- *Offers help without taking responsibility away from those who are truly accountable*

- *Shares thoughts with the team or individual about what needs to be done and then asks for voluntary participation with no strings attached*

- *Lets others learn from their mistakes without judgment*

- *Is a resource, not a supervisor, and does not own the outcome*

- *Provides outside support services for the good of everyone*

"So often that's true, Pete. But in freedom-based organizations, the job description changes. Leaders learn to wait to be asked and become resources to their people—they no longer just barge in."

"Kip, is there a quick example you can share with me on an operation that learned how to behave like this?"

"Sure, Johnsonville Foods, headquartered in the Upper Midwest of the United States, provides a good example of an operation that behaves with freedom-based leadership. The company grew under this new leadership approach by twentyfold within a half dozen years. Leaders at every level learned to wait to be asked. At Johnsonville, the old frontline supervisors evolved into Wise Counsels. With the help of these Wise Counsels, frontline employees learned to do their own planning, scheduling, budgeting, and even hiring and firing."[2]

"Were you able to emulate Johnsonville at National Stores, Kip?"

"You bet we were," said Kip, with obvious pride, "but it took lots and lots of work, Pete. We completely discarded the popular notion of a strong leader as someone who sticks to his guns, a commanding-general/godlike figure, someone to be revered and feared.[3]

"A Wise Counsel understands that flexibility and openness are actually much more powerful than control. Rather than imposing rigid policies and procedures, our leaders learned to encourage their staff to follow the Johnsonville and Nordstrom models of using their own good judgment in dealing with customers, in making decisions, and in solving problems. We recognized that more controls and rules weren't the answer.

"And note that I no longer ever refer to our leaders as 'managers,'" clarified Kip. "This is because our leaders no longer manage people, nor do they want to. Once we explained to our leadership and staff the implications of what it meant to be a manager and to have a manager, no one wanted any part of the manager role or a manager–employee relationship.

"At National Stores, there were a few control-addicted managers and supervisors who were unable to make the transition. Some simply couldn't give up the need to control. But after good faith attempts, each of those supervisors and I had a 'This is not working out' conversation.

"As the senior executive at National Stores, I bore the responsibility for asking a manager or supervisor to leave the organization. Staff members hadn't hired the supervisor. I had in a direct or indirect way, and so I believed I owned that responsibility. Thank goodness I didn't have to do it very often!"

Pete nodded in understanding.

"We learned," continued Kip, "that we really couldn't empower anyone. We could disempower others, however, whenever we gave in to our fears and our need to control. Rather than relying on position, politics, experience, or title to establish power and authority, as had previously been the case at National Stores, we taught people that they already possessed the power to get the job done, and we were only there to help. It took longer than we'd hoped, but it did happen."

Kip, after pausing and reflecting a moment, said proudly, "It was magnificent to see when it started to take hold in our operations all over the country."

"I bet it was," Pete said with a smile, "but what if people needed assistance?"

"If they did, all they needed to do was ask," answered Kip. "By asking for help and not faking it, mistakes were reduced by the hundreds!"

"At my company," interjected Pete, "mistakes by the hundreds are driving us crazy and costing us millions!"

Kip nodded, understanding firsthand what Pete was talking about. "Thoughtless mistakes drove our management team crazy, too, until we figured out that we needed to stay out of the way and wait to be asked."

"Waiting to be asked sounds very passive," observed Pete skeptically.

"It isn't passive at all! We were very active," responded Kip. "Our job was to get our people to develop their own Keen Internal Vision—a vision of what needed to be done. That's not anything like the slogans of a company vision. No, the Keen Internal Vision is a one-on-one relationship between you and your job, and it takes some energy and time to define that relationship.

The Keen Internal Vision is a one-on-one relationship between you and your job.

"Here's an example of what I mean. Let's say you work in a control-based company, and it's three o'clock. You look at the clock and think to yourself, 'Hum . . . I have two more hours to go, then I'm out of here.' OK, now let's change the context of the situation: same person, same time of day, but this time you work in a freedom-based company and run your own little operation, and everything depends on your efforts. Now, when you look at the clock you say, 'My heavens, it's already three o'clock!' implying that you have so many things to do and so little time."

"I get it, Kip," smiled Pete. "With a Keen Internal Vision of your ownership, time or even the activities you are a part of take on a different meaning."

Kip nodded and offered another example. "Let me relate a true story from history that suggests that a Keen Internal Vision can have very serious consequences for an organization or, in this case, a country." He paused and then began.

"In 1961, when John F. Kennedy put forth the idea of sending a man to the moon and bringing him back safely to Earth before the end of the decade, the American people were stirred by his vision.

"But Congress was not so sure. We were in a death struggle with the Russians, deep in the Cold War, and we couldn't afford the loss of face. Both Democrats and Republicans were afraid that the United States would fail in its attempt and that this failure—of our technological power—would be seen on television around the world.

"Senator George Smathers of Florida, a good friend of Kennedy's, was part of a congressional team sent to Cape Canaveral to determine whether funding for the project should be appropriated. During a tour of the grounds, Senator Smathers happened upon a woman sweeping up after hours in one of the huge hangars. With his coat flung over his back and his tie loosened, he began chatting with the woman and eventually asked her, 'What do you do here?'

"Her answer showed her deep understanding of her personal Keen Internal Vision and the vision of NASA—our national aerospace agency. It was her fateful words that affected not only the Florida senator but the future of space exploration—and she wasn't even a scientist or astronaut."

"What could she have possibly said that would have caused such a powerful response from Smathers?" asked Pete, enthralled with Kip's story.

"Here's what she said: *'I'm part of a team helping to get a man to the moon and back home safely.'*" Kip paused to let the depth of the meaning set in and then said, "With that, Senator Smathers returned to Washington where he cast the deciding vote to fund the moon project—and the rest, as they say, is history."

"Wow! So, a cleaning woman understood that her simple job of sweeping up was an important part of the moon project," said Pete.

"It turned out that she wasn't that insignificant or unimportant," remarked Kip. "No, Smathers reasoned that after this woman's fateful comment, it was logical to assume that everyone at NASA saw themselves as a team member of a powerful shared vision—a national mission of great importance.

"If getting to the moon had become a personal mission for this cleaning woman, imagine what it meant to some of the key players. Smathers recognized the power of a shared Keen Internal Vision. He knew that this advantage would mean the difference between success and failure—that much he *knew*," said Kip smiling.

"Imagine if she had simply said, 'Huh? What does it look like I do?'" said Pete. "We might today have a Russian flag on the moon."

"Quite possibly," said Kip, with a pronounced smile of irony on his face.

"One person can sure make a difference," observed Pete.

"You bet!" said the older man. "Pete, certainly one person can make a difference, but everyone working together is vastly more powerful. Once everyone shares a Keen Internal Vision, they start thinking about how by performing their job to the best of their ability, they can help make the vision a reality—and that's a wonderfully energizing experience! We start with the individual, connect one individual to other empowered individuals, and before you know it we have a critical mass!" said Kip with outstretched arms.

"Pete, the purpose of the internal vision is to give people the individual freedom they need. By doing this, we allow them to take personal responsibility for their choices, and that's how you create the context to achieve true accountability."

The purpose of the internal vision is to give people the individual freedom they need. By doing this, we allow them to take personal responsibility for their choices, and that's how you create the context to achieve true accountability.

"OK, so I understand about the Keen Internal Vision and the two examples you gave, but how do Wise Counsels make things happen, especially since they're supposed to wait to be asked?" inquired Pete.

"We weren't sitting in our offices," answered Kip. "We Wise Counsels spent more than half of our time teaching and coaching. In this new environment, the vast majority of people at National Stores quickly became capable of taking responsibility and of being accountable. We were always there, but we weren't in anyone's face or on anyone's back! By providing advice when asked, we demonstrated respect, support, and care for our staff members."

Pete interjected, "Didn't you find that what people want is not always what will make them successful?"

"Yes," responded Kip, "but by developing a relationship of mutual respect, our people learned to trust our good intentions even when we weren't able to give them what they wanted. In the beginning, we weren't perfect; we made mistakes—boy, did we make mistakes! But because our egos weren't attached to our coaching and we weren't keeping score, people could see that our intentions were good. We learned and learned and learned until we got it right.

"Additionally, at National Stores, we Wise Counsels had to learn to let go of our fears."

"What kind of fears?" asked Pete.

"Well, for one, the fear that people would take advantage of us," answered Kip. "Human nature being what it is proved that there were a few people who tried to take advantage of us, but they were few in number, and we dealt with them in an appropriate and professional fashion. Surprisingly, in most cases, peers took care of these folks without our intervention. It was amazing."

"So you trusted everyone?" asked Pete with disbelief.

"Our choices were pretty clear," Kip continued. "Either we were going to trust no one until they earned it, or we were going to trust everyone until they proved to be untrustworthy.

"The problem with the first strategy is that trust was rarely earned in the way we expect it to be. We recognized that the former approach creates a college fraternity hazing mentality instead of a meaningful, trusting relationship.

"Pete, the advantage of the second strategy is that by extending trust to everyone—right from the onset—trust is nearly always returned in kind. That's the lesson we learned.

"Even if we were sometimes disappointed, we concluded that it was far better to be occasionally disappointed than to trust no one and foster a climate of mutual distrust, which would put us back into a control-based environment.

"As the intentions of the leadership at National Stores became clear and as people saw us truly letting go of our need to control, people began to trust us more and to ask for what they really needed."

"But how did people know what to ask for?" questioned Pete.

"The key to that challenge is in getting everyone in the organization to understand and internalize their Keen Internal

Vision," replied Kip, "or, put another way, how their efforts fit into the big picture, just like the cleaning woman at NASA.

"We spent a lot of time up-front letting everyone know what we were up to. I didn't believe that we had a bunch of mind readers, so I continued to drive home the point that you can't expect people to know what's on your mind—you've got to tell them. And you have to find creative ways to do that every chance you get.

"Such chances I call 'teachable moments.' Simply put, teachable moments are opportunities to tell or teach someone something new or to reiterate an idea or principle. Most often teachable moments are centered around our values or our beliefs. And, by the way, using a teachable moment approach works equally well at home and with your extended family and friends."

Teachable moments are opportunities to tell or teach someone something new or to reiterate an idea or principle.

"It sounds like *owning* your job is another key ingredient in creating a freedom-based organization," reasoned Pete.

"Right again Pete," affirmed Kip. "In a freedom-based environment, responsibility and accountability lie with those closest to the tasks. By crafting this notion, we actually inverted the pyramid. That is, we put the point of the pyramid downward. Instead of the boss being on top, we flipped the diagram and placed the customer on top. Just below the customer is the frontline person serving that customer. Senior leadership supports the staff workers who own the jobs and serve the customers, but the frontline people call the shots, not impersonal policies and not supervisors.

"Even though we are in retail, the activity is the same as it would be in a service or manufacturing environment. We place the customer in contact with the manufacturing team that is responsible for the finished product; this includes both internal and external customers. In the service industry, the customer and the service provider make the transaction.

"The application of this philosophy is well known in the quality movement. But here's the catch. When this approach is applied in a control-based environment, it will not work long-term because of the accountability of supervision and the lack of accountability of the frontline worker. It works beautifully in a freedom-based context where it is both actionable and sustainable."

Pete took Kip's comments and continued with them. "So, owning your job is a concept that allows staff members to completely let go of the idea that they need someone to look to for direction or control. Rather, this new approach assumes that everyone is capable of managing himself or herself and that owning one's job is a key success factor to a business's survival."

"Exactly, Pete," Kip nodded. "The freedom-based philosophy assumes that together with others and in consideration of the needs of the organization, you can set your own goals and be accountable for the results. This concept," he added, "completely lets go of the notion that you're accountable to people in authority.

"Remember, we literally stripped the organization of supervision. We got rid of the position and the role, not the people who held those positions. A freedom-based workplace is not a strategy to flatten the operation. Flat operations are still in a control-based mode. No, this is very different in intent.

"Owning your job takes the place of the supervisor. Now the individual is the boss. And by creating this context, each staff member becomes accountable to the whole organization and to his or her customers, both the internal and external ones. That's the key strategy in creating long-term value."

"You know, you're right, Kip," concurred Pete. "I've been working with the Japanese for the past several years and have observed this kind of accountability. I always assumed it was cultural and unique to the Japanese."

"Pete, it's not about being Japanese or any nationality," countered Kip. "At first, there was an inordinately large number of people at National Stores who seemed incapable of accepting responsibility and accountability. But we learned that these individuals were not incapable; most simply refused to accept responsibility in the dangerous environment of the past. Remember, that was a time when we forced accountability on people, so we had a lot of work ahead of us.

Owning your job takes the place of the supervisor. Now the individual is the boss. And by creating this context, each staff member becomes accountable to the whole organization and to his or her customers, both the internal and external ones. That's the key strategy in creating long-term value.

"As the CEO, I decided that whatever happened, we weren't going back to the old days. No, sir, we weren't going to let anyone or anything drag us back to the way we used to think or act, and that commitment was key."

"Kip, this seems to be an important point," declared Pete. "From what you're saying, I shouldn't expect that our people will immediately jump at the chance to be responsible even after we've announced our intentions of becoming freedom based. Every manager and supervisor has to hold the course and not blink!"

"That was my experience, Pete," remarked Kip. "You may even hear many of your people, when they learn about this new philosophy and approach, say, 'If you want me to be responsible, then pay me like a manager.' There were people at National who had developed patterns of behavior that led them away from accepting responsibility. They were full-blown entitlement junkies—'Gimme, gimme, gimme' was their answer to everything, especially any changes we wanted to attempt.

"Yet our experience showed that most people, even those who were reluctant to accept responsibility, were capable of being responsible, provided they were treated with respect, patience, and trust.

"Not everyone on the staff came to this new approach easily or quickly. Some did, but most sat on the sidelines and waited for us to blink and to go back to the old ways.

"But we didn't blink, and they eventually became believers. My attitude became, 'I will not change back to the old ways and will hold to this new belief about the way to treat people until hell freezes over!'" Both men laughed, but Pete got the message—don't blink!

Pete asked, "What about those who never got it?"

"The few people who were unable to meet our new expectations," answered Kip, "ultimately left the organization, usually of their own accord. In fact, we lost only about 2 percent of our total staff, not the 5 percent I had talked about earlier.[4] I'm confident that you'll have the same experience at your company.

"Overall, our turnover was significantly reduced when we moved to a freedom-based approach. Once we had staff members hiring staff members, our world changed for the good. It's funny, but the staff's perception of candidates was far different than that of supervisors."

"I think I know why you got better at hiring the right people," reflected Pete. "I bet your staff members realized that they now had more at stake if the wrong person was let in. After all, frontline people had to depend on each other. But how do you deal with individuals who won't leave on their own and who continue to refuse to accept personal responsibility and accountability?"

Kip lowered his voice and fixed his gaze on Pete: "You must be direct and fair. As the new standards become widely understood and practiced, no one can remain exempt. When the code of accountability to the organization is broken, the organization, not individual members, bears the responsibility for administering justice."

"When you say the organization, you mean the leadership, don't you?" inquired Pete.

"That's one of the burdens of leadership at every level, Pete," said Kip. "In the future, as the staff begins to hire, then the responsibilities in this area change. But that's not going to happen for you in the first several years. In the beginning this responsibility will fall on you and your fellow executives' shoulders."

Even with all the information Kip was sharing, Pete continued to be skeptical. "It seems pie-in-the-sky to believe that people at every level of the organization in my company are capable of accepting personal responsibility and of being accountable."

Kip countered, "It may seem hard to believe, but our experience at National Stores was that personal responsibility and being accountable became commonplace—they became the norm! As people at National Stores began to understand and accept the concept of freedom with accountability, they became inoculated against the diseases of fear, irresponsibility, apathy, and the need to control others."

"OK, Kip, so I understand that most people learn to be accountable and that part of owning your job is being accountable to your customers, but how did you keep people focused on customers while all this change was occurring?" asked Pete.

"Nowadays, most organizations claim to be consumer oriented or, another name that's used, customer centered," responded Kip with a grin, "yet, when examined closely, it becomes apparent that control-based organizational structures, perhaps originally designed to serve the customer, have fossilized into inflexible and impenetrable bureaucracies."

"I know what you mean," agreed Pete. "Recently, I had my wife's car serviced, and I wanted to talk to the mechanic who serviced the car. Do you know what the service people said?" asked Pete.

"I think I do," smiled Kip.

"They said I couldn't talk to him," said Pete. "That's not what I call customer service. That's what I call an iron curtain. And yet this garage prides itself on customer service!"

"Pete, that's a perfect example. Our old control-based management systems at National Stores used organizational structures to constrain people to the tasks assigned to them by those of us in authority. While these restrictions were intended to make the people operating within them more accountable, in fact, the restrictions frequently rendered our people incapable of servicing the customer.

"If what the customer wanted was outside the parameters of our processes and policies, our employees could do nothing for them without approval from their boss's boss." Kip just shook his head and continued.

"This is where Lucy and her associates miss the boat and where their processes naturally break down. We realized, in living color, that once we made the change to a freedom-based approach, one size didn't fit all customers.

"And so the best policy in many cases is this: Trust your people to do the right thing by the customer, and take every opportunity to encourage your people to serve customers, as they would wish to be served."

> *The best policy in many cases is this:*
> *Trust your people to do the right thing,*
> *and take every opportunity to encourage*
> *your people to serve customers, as*
> *they would wish to be served.*

"That's a universal policy we can all follow," said Pete in a congratulatory tone. "In fact, isn't that similar to the approach the world-famous Ritz Carlton takes: 'We are ladies and gentlemen serving ladies and gentlemen.'"

Kip nodded and went on, recognizing the quote Pete had just related. "At National Stores, we learned that the more managers and supervisors relied on control-based job descriptions, systems, and policies to define what their people did, the more people avoided anything that was not within the policies or their job descriptions. And the reason was simple—in our old environment people didn't want to foul up for fear of incurring the boss's wrath or facing the music at the semiannual performance review. In short, we learned that a control-based job description is a description of what an employee *doesn't* do!"

A control-based job description is a description of what an employee doesn't do!

This point gave Kip a wonderful opening to rail about another subject that had been stuck in his craw for years. "And a word about performance reviews, if you'll allow me a moment to vent," he said. "We came to believe performance reviews were the worst idea since debtor's prison."

Pete laughed out loud.

Kip continued, chuckling along with Pete. "Here's what we realized: If our people were focusing on pleasing the boss, they weren't paying the right kind of attention to their customers!"

"Kip," Pete broke in, "in my experience, even in a control-based environment, resourceful people figure out that it's better to ask for forgiveness than to ask for permission."

"You're right on that point," Kip acknowledged. "What was more devastating to National Stores, however, was that under the old control-based structures, our people tended to force customers into complying with *our* company policies—which were designed for our convenience, not for our customers' needs. Using phrases like, 'I'm sorry, our company policy doesn't allow us to do what you request,' caused our own employees to destroy our goodwill with our customers.

"In the waning days of our old control-base culture," Kip continued, "I was getting customer complaints about what our people thought they *couldn't* do. If I'd sat up nights with comedy writers, I couldn't have come up with loonier stories about how we were killing our relationships with our precious customers.

"Well, we put an end to these policies in short order. The really scary thing was that in the old days, we wouldn't have considered these customer complaints valid; we'd have considered these customers, well, unreasonable."

"I guess it's all about what point of view you're coming from."

Kip reflected on Pete's comment and continued with his confession. "Rather than risking punishment from those of us at the top, who had created the policies out of a sincere desire to be customer centered, these policies had become customer service monsters! In short, this approach had become the kiss of death for our organization. It wasn't until after my heart attack, when I finally faced my fear of letting go and of trusting, that National Stores began to turn around.

"As we moved toward becoming a freedom-based organization, we rebuilt all our organizational structures around the customer. We came to say that the biggest sacred cows made the best hamburgers. We even had a barbecue to celebrate the changes we were making to our systems!"

Pete laughed along with Kip. "Kip, what were your sacred cows?"

"First, one of our biggest and juiciest—hierarchies were discarded in order to maximize customer contact with the people who directly served them. And, second, every internal function was arranged to serve the customer. The design question we asked was, 'How should we organize to make it easy for customers to do business with us?'

"We came to realize that if we wanted everyone at National Stores to be accountable and to make well-crafted decisions, they needed to see the world from the customer's perspective and not get this perspective secondhand from a manager or even a Wise Counsel.

"In a freedom-based workplace, the staff needs to know how the customer sees the organization. Staying in the back room is a flawed approach. Everyone needs to get involved if they are to be accountable. Isolating members of the staff on a need-to-know basis works in a control-based environment where you want people to be compliant, but it's a real liability in a freedom-based workplace where you need staff members to advocate creative solutions and approaches.

"For example," Kip went on, "while in the past we had restricted customer contact to the sales and service departments, as a freedom-based organization we began to involve our customers in research and development of some of our products. We even manufactured some of our products to a unique set of customer specifications. Some customers controlled and monitored how and when we shipped them product.

In a freedom-based workplace, the staff needs to know how the customer sees the organization.

"We instituted a program that put our product managers in the stores selling to our customers three days per month—something they never did before. By doing so, product managers were able to hear firsthand from the customers how the merchandise was being interpreted by the customer and what problems customers were having with the 'shopping experience.'

"We even created opportunities for our warehouse people to wait on customers directly—and, boy, was that an eye-opener for them. In addition, we let salespeople make the call on what to do with a customer return or complaint. No longer did our salespeople have to get permission. Instead, we asked our salespeople to use their good judgment. Sound familiar?

"In the end, we had numerous customer-centered process groups that included one or more representatives from each of our internal functions. Some of these groups existed for months, others for only a few hours, depending on the needs of the customer.

"This new, highly flexible organizational structure allowed our people to serve as members of several process groups at one time, while being a resource to others. Of course, accomplishing this kind of structural change required the full participation and commitment of people throughout the organization to design and take responsibility for maintaining them. In the end, building highly flexible structures that were truly customer centered is what allowed us to become incredibly competitive."

"How did all of these changes affect profits?" asked Pete.

"We didn't ignore our profits. We shared our numbers with all our employees and found out something very interesting: People needed to be educated on how to read a balance sheet and a profit-and-loss statement. For the first time in over seventy years, our people at every level knew our profit-and-loss picture, and, boy, was that an eye-opener for them and for us.

"Our people learned to care about profits, whereas before they only cared about their salary and what was in it for them. They learned to connect the dots between company profits and customer satisfaction. Our profit picture and our ability to respond to changes in the market improved measurably. We stopped using extrinsic incentives, but we still recognized outstanding performance. And, as far as policies went, we reduced them to one piece of paper. No longer did we ask people to do things right; now we asked them to do the right thing. That made all the difference in the world!

"Pete, none of what we accomplished at National Stores would have been possible without great people: people who craved individual freedom, who were eager to accept personal responsibility, and who demanded accountability from everyone in the organization. Let me tell you what we looked for in great people.

No longer did we ask people to do things right; now we asked them to do the right thing. That made all the difference in the world!

"Great people recognize each other for what they contribute, but not in a way that gives credit to one person while ignoring the contribution of others. They're willing to take personal risks if it will benefit the organization and are willing to tell the truth even when the truth is hard to share. Great people extend trust to everyone, withholding it from no one. They are open to new ideas and are willing to experiment, even when they initially disagree.

"Great people have high standards of integrity; they wouldn't think of touching a dishonest dollar. They're willing to put the interests of others first, believing that doing so is not only good for the organization but good for them personally. Putting the interests of others first proved to be the glue that bound our great people to one another and created a healthy community at National Stores."

Great People

- Recognize each other for what they contribute.
- Take personal risks if it will benefit the organization.
- Are willing to tell the truth even when the truth is hard to share.
- Extend trust to everyone.
- Are open to new ideas.
- Are willing to experiment, even when they initially disagree.
- Have high standards of integrity.
- Do not touch dishonest dollars.
- Are willing to put the interests of others first.

"How did you ever find people like that, Kip?" inquired Pete.

"In most cases they were already working for us. What we learned was that when you create a freedom-based work environment, people just naturally respond by being their best. You see, Pete, people really do want to be great. They just need a place where they're free to behave that way!"

Pete's head was awash with new ideas, and he was ready for a break. So when the steward knocked on their door, he welcomed the interruption.

The sun hovered just over the horizon as it broke through the storm clouds for the first time that day. Streaks of pink and gold reached out like long fingers across the new-fallen snow. The hills cast long shadows across the valley as the engine pushed aside the snow that lay across the tracks.

11

Creating the Right Conditions

The steward knocked softly at the compartment door. Opening it, he said, "Gentlemen, I reserved a table for you as you requested, and the two ladies seemed pleased to join you. Your table is ready now if you'd like to follow me."

The two men followed the steward back to the dining car where they were seated in a spacious booth. Yolanda was already seated at the table.

"Hello, gentlemen—thanks for inviting me," she smiled. "You saved me from a fate worse than death." All three laughed as they began to speak about Hank Striker and his approach to managing people.

Yolanda looked at the two men. "You're not going to believe what I went through. I was about to jump out of the window or slash my wrists, and then the steward came and said that you wanted me to join you. I must apologize for my initial reaction to what you were saying earlier today." She looked at Kip and smiled, obviously somewhat embarrassed.

"Not a problem," said Kip in an amicable tone. "I do understand where you're coming from, and your reactions to my earlier comments are pretty normal. I'm used to getting strong reactions," he added with a warm and friendly smile.

"So, Yolanda, tell us—what was it like to be locked up with Striker for almost four hours?" asked Pete in a teasing tone.

"The guy's like a bull in a china shop. I mean, he must have learned his people skills from Genghis Khan. He told me he's on his fourth wife."

"Only four?" said Pete, laughing.

"Don't laugh—he tried to talk me into becoming number five!" said Yolanda, joking. "Seems he's a big shot in Cleveland, Ohio, where he owns and operates a large parts manufacturing plant for the bathroom and plumbing industry. He built it from scratch and works one hundred hours per week holding onto his empire—says he signs every check. Claims people are stealing from him, so he has guards and lockdown procedures every night. He was complaining about some recent lawsuit. He hates lawyers and politicians. Says they're all crooks." Pete shook his head in disbelief.

"What's the name of his company?" asked Kip, trying to keep the conversation light.

"I think he said it was Friendly Plumbing or something like that," replied Yolanda in a serious tone, not realizing the irony.

"That may be the biggest oxymoron in Cleveland!" chortled Pete.

"I've heard of them," said Kip, trying to keep the character assassinations to a minimum. "I started my career in Cleveland. It's a friendly town."

"So did you sell him an incentive program?" needled Pete good-naturedly, not taking Kip's conciliatory lead.

"Almost," winked Yolanda.

"Hi, everyone," said a woman's voice.

"Hi, Lucy," said Pete. "Glad you could join us. Yolanda was bringing us up to speed on our cigar-chomping friend, Hank Striker. And you won't believe the name of his company."

"You've got to be kidding! You're in Striker's compartment?" looking at Yolanda with amusement. "Gee, some people have all the luck!" said Lucy.

By now, only the dim lights of an occasional distant farmhouse were visible outside the dining car window. When the waiter appeared at their table, Kip, who knew

the menu by heart, made suggestions to the other three peo-
ple. Trusting Kip's judgment, everyone ordered.

Lucy, all at once, turned to Kip and picked up the conversation where they'd left it several hours earlier: "I've been
thinking about your comments at lunch. I'd like to know
more about your experience at National Stores; I'm always
open to new ideas. I know there are limitations to any program, including ours, and I'd like to hear more about freedom-based environments. Tell me about where you start?"

Kip nodded. Pete welcomed the request. He'd expected a
more social conversation, but this was perfect.

Kip, concerned with her earlier reaction to this topic,
turned to Yolanda and asked, "If I answer Lucy's question,
would that be OK? I know you weren't thrilled with my comments at lunch."

"Are you kidding?" said Yolanda, with a wide grin. "I owe
all of you big-time for saving me from Hank. And, besides, at
lunch I wasn't ready to admit that you might be right. I still
believe in my product. Incentives can make a difference, and
I mean that, but I need to be more open-minded. It seemed
that the three of you were a lot more on track with each
other, and I was the odd man out. Maybe there's something
to what you said, Kip. I just don't know."

She turned to Pete and said, "Time heals all wounds—except the wounds Striker inflicted on me in the passenger
compartment." Everyone laughed at Yolanda's joke, and they
appreciated her new openness.

"Great!" said Kip. "But, first, I need to ask a delicate question." Looking at Lucy, he asked, "Why are you interested in
this subject?"

"Kip," began Lucy, "I know my projects have problems,
but I always thought that was normal. Now I'm not sure. And
the problems seem to have a common theme—that is the
most troubling aspect. We start off great with our clients, but
then something happens around the fourth or fifth month.

"We start to get pushback from the managers and from
the staff. My boss and the other top consultants in the firm
almost seem to expect this pushback. Our solution, as you

know, is a systems response. But there's something missing, and earlier today you made sense. I couldn't help thinking about when my brother played for a triple A baseball team in the early nineties. He had bad knees that finally ended his career. But before that, they would shoot him up with medication that numbed his knees. Sometimes, I feel that's what we're doing to our clients—numbing them up.

"It's hard to deny your thesis or the research that supports your argument. I've read some of the same case studies in the business review magazines, but I never connected the dots before today.

"I'm not surrendering—well, at least not just yet," she said, smiling, and continued. "No white flag or anything like that, but I do want to hear more. Who knows, if you convince me, I might become your partner and fight the good fight. Of course, I'd need a bonus," she added half-jokingly.

Pete was taking this conversation all in. He saw before him two very smart people who were beginning to open up to the possibility that a freedom-based approach might work. Yolanda was interpreting Kip's ideas from a behaviorist's viewpoint, and Lucy was looking at it from a systems' perspective. He was looking at it from a CEO's vantage point— no one was discounting the freedom-based idea anymore. And the interesting part was the huge divergence of their initial perspectives. "These two women aren't 100 percent on board," Pete thought, "but they are no longer fighting with Kip. They want to learn more and then make up their own minds."

He'd learned over the years that women have a special knack for processing information differently than men. He knew that the best adviser he'd ever had was his wife because she would tell him the truth—even when it hurt. These two businesswomen were interested in what Kip had to say, and they were sharp cookies; they weren't pushovers. Thirty percent of his management team was women and would probably react in the same way these two experienced women had. He expected them to, and he needed the data points if he was going to be successful in creating change in his environment.

"As Kip and I were talking candidly so far today," Pete said, "he was telling me about his brother and how he overcame his alcohol addiction." He looked at Kip for an OK, and Kip nodded his support of where Pete was going with his comments.

"Kip said something that made all the sense in the world. He told me that you first have to admit to yourself that you're out of control. And, once you admit you have a problem, you can begin exploring your choices. I think that's what I just heard from you two ladies, and I'm with you on this."

Pete took a deep breath and then said, "I have a giant business problem at my company, and it's all about not being able to get my people to become accountable for their performance.

"Until this train ride and today's specific conversation, I frankly didn't have the guts to face the fact that what we've been doing isn't working. Now, I'm ready to admit it!" Pete needed to get this off his chest and believed this forum was both the right time and the right place.

"Also, I've been feeling the pressure of being a CEO—something I've worked all my life to achieve. But I'm not willing to have a heart attack to force needed changes."

At this point, Kip interrupted, saying, "I think he's referring to my wake-up call around twenty years ago—my own heart attack. That's how I got the message about the freedom-based approach to leading people."

Pete continued, while looking at Kip: "The personal experiences you've related, the evidence you've shared, and my own reading confirms what I've quietly thought for a long time: that my organization needs a new approach. Now I'm hearing Yolanda and Lucy express interest in these ideas as well. So I welcome this conversation and all your company.

"I'm ready to begin the journey toward a freedom-based operation; I just hope I have the courage to see it through! I know I asked this before, Kip, but, can you give me more details about how I begin?" At that Pete smiled and fell silent.

Kip looked at his three companions and said, "First, you've got to create the right conditions for the freedom-based philosophy to take hold. The right conditions are what enable great people to do great work. It took us upward of two years to install the strategies required to establish the right conditions."

"But how do the right conditions improve operational results?" questioned Pete.

"In an environment where interpersonal tension is low, where groups work well together, and where responsibility is shared appropriately, improvements in operational results are not only possible but inevitable. And you don't have to wait two years to see results. We began seeing results as soon as we started employing the very first strategy. Let me share a story that illustrates the power of having the right conditions."

His three companions looked relaxed yet focused on Kip.

"Campers, hikers, and hunters," Kip began, "have long known that if they want a lantern they can rely on, they have only to buy a Coleman lantern. One day, old man Coleman, the founder of the company, showed up at the office—even though he was retired—for a production meeting. Upon his arrival, the group was discussing what to do about a defective gas jet that leaked under pressure in one of their products. The question before the group was whether the company, famed for its impeccable quality, publicly admit the defect and launch a product recall.

"It was April, and there were several thousand of the defective units already on store shelves, and the camping season was just around the corner. The production staff estimated that only a small proportion of the lanterns were thought to have the defective jet. One marketing person argued, 'With so few bad units, and with the cost of a recall so high, why not wait for customers to return the defective products?'

"Up until that moment, Mr. Coleman had been listening quietly, which was his rule of behavior, but this last comment was too much. He slammed the table with his fist and bellowed, 'What's the matter with you people? Don't you understand that every Coleman lantern has to work?'

"To Mr. Coleman, the company's values were clear. They had built a company where their Shared Values demanded that a defective product be recalled immediately! Coleman customers had come to depend on the reliability of the product, and he was not about to sacrifice their hundred-year, hard-earned trust for any reason."

Yolanda asked, "So, one of the conditions to build this kind of workplace is the bedrock values an operation has, isn't it?"

"Yes," said Kip.

"But you called it something special, didn't you?" asked Lucy.

"Kip called it 'Shared Values,' right?" interjected Pete.

Kip took the cue. "Yes, that's what I called it. Shared Values are a part of the Keen Internal Vision of an operation. They are the bedrock values that Yolanda was referring to. A Keen Internal Vision is nothing more than the road map each individual uses to navigate through the dangers we all face every day, recognizing that we all face a political environment as well as a job-related environment."

A Keen Internal Vision is nothing more than the road map each individual uses to navigate through the dangers we face every day, recognizing that we all face a political environment as well as a job-related environment.

"Sure, and it was the reputation of the business that was at stake that Coleman responded to," said Pete.

"No wonder he was angry," said Lucy. They all nodded.

"'The wrong conditions lead people to do the wrong thing. The right conditions lead people to behave ethically,'"[1] said Kip. "Remember, treating people ethically creates loyalty, and loyalty leads to accountability."

"And you can't create an incentive program that would accomplish that, can you?" asked Yolanda. Kip shook his head.

"So an organization's Shared Values create the conditions for ethical behavior!" said Lucy emphatically.

Kip looked at Lucy expectantly, encouraging her to continue her thought. "Now here's a very interesting idea," he said, "and it dovetails well with the kinds of systems you want to put in place, Lucy. The idea goes something like this: Ethical behavior is less dependent on whether the people themselves are predisposed to be ethical than it is on the conditions in which they find themselves, and this runs counter to what many people believe."

"OK, so you create a system that promotes ethical behavior," said Yolanda, "but how do you do that without incentives?"

"Or without a set of policies or rules?" asked Lucy.

Pete smiled, waiting for Kip's answer. These two women had tag-teamed Kip again.

Ethical behavior is less dependent on whether the people themselves are predisposed to be ethical than it is on the conditions in which they find themselves, and this runs counter to what many people believe.

Kip welcomed the challenge. "To answer that, I need to get somewhat clinical for a moment. I'm going to use two criminologists, James Q. Wilson and George Kelling, to explain how you do it," he said, looking to Yolanda and then Lucy. These two researchers call their theory the 'broken windows theory,' and it's all about context."

"We use that term as well in our work," said Lucy. "Context is a powerful element in people's perceptions. Context is our reality, isn't it?"

"Yes, that is exactly correct," said Kip. "Wilson and Kelling's theory applies to building a freedom-based environment, and I think you'll find their argument intriguing, if not enlightening. Unfortunately, their thesis can be applied in both constructive and destructive ways, so it's doubly important to learn this lesson well if you're going to begin the journey of building a freedom-based workplace."

Kip continued, saying, "Wilson and Kelling argue that crime is the inevitable result of disorder. If a window is broken and left broken, people walking by will conclude that no one cares and no one is in charge. Soon more windows will be broken, and the sense of anarchy will spread from the building to the street on which it faces, sending a signal that anything goes. In a city, relatively minor problems like graffiti, public disorder, and aggressive panhandling are all the equivalent of broken windows, invitations to more serious crimes.[2]

Wilson and Kelling argue that crime is the inevitable result of disorder. If a window is broken and left broken, people walking by will conclude that no one cares and no one is in charge. . . . In a city, relatively minor problems like graffiti, public disorder, and aggressive panhandling are all the equivalent of broken windows, invitations to more serious crimes.

Kip paused for a moment, and Pete jumped in before he could continue. "You're saying that the broken windows theory compares crime to disease, suggesting that crime is contagious," said Pete.

"Exactly," said Kip. "It's not the presence of potential criminals, they conclude, that leads to a crime wave, because these elements are always present. Rather, the power of context is the cause."

"OK," said Yolanda. "Let me see if I can capture this idea. Once the right conditions are present, criminal behavior blossoms? So if you create the right conditions, accountability will blossom? Is that what you're saying?"

"Yes, that's what the theory says," said Kip, "and that's the way you create any sustainable change. But it takes constant work and energy, just like keeping crime off the street."

Lucy added, "So if the conditions of social decay can lead to a crime wave, then the reverse might be true as well? Is that what you're arguing?"

Kip nodded, and Lucy said, "I see."

"I find this very interesting, but do you have numbers to support it?" asked Pete.

Nodding, Kip replied, "I sure do. A leading American research organization has collected data over the past twelve years on organizational conditions from over two thousand global sites, not just in the United States. The data from this study, called the Values & Attitude Study (VAS), when correlated with measures of operational results, such as turnover rate, productivity, and profitability, demonstrate a direct link between healthy conditions and improvements in these same critical measures.

"The study trends also show that as the work environment improves; that is, as the workplace becomes more freedom-based, so too does accountability improve. In other words, healthy work environments—freedom-based environments—create the right conditions for people to be accountable. Put simply, happy people are more productive, and the data quantifiably confirm this correlation.[3]

"The broken windows theory and the VAS numerical data suggest that 'we are more than just sensitive to changes in context. We're exquisitely sensitive to them.'"[4]

Lucy, trying to clarify her thoughts, asked, "Kip, so you're saying the data from several reliable sources suggest that by making even small changes in the social conditions, big changes in individual and group behavior can occur without any systems changes or incentive programs?"

By making even small changes in the social conditions, big changes in individual and group behavior can occur without any systems changes or incentive programs.

"Yes, I am," said Kip, as he repeated himself for emphasis. "Yes, I am!"

Just then, the waiter appeared with plates of salads, placed them in front of the four travelers, and said, "Folks, your dinners will be right up!" As Yolanda and the others sprinkled pepper on their crisp greens, Kip continued.

"Let me share another story of an organization in Minneapolis with which I've personally worked, Ault Inc. Ault's top leaders had already invested two-plus years in crafting their freedom-based workplace when this particular crisis hit them. As I relate the experience, see if you think that the typical organization that was not freedom-based would have reacted as Ault did."

"So, they acted the way they did because they were freedom based?" asked Lucy.

Kip shook his head yes as he took a bite of his salad.

"What happened?" asked Pete.

The older man wiped his mouth with the white cotton napkin and said, "Ault is a manufacturing firm that had about 165 employees when this incident took place. Its executives were in the process of obtaining an increase in Ault's line of credit from the bank. This credit expansion was crucial for sustaining operations at a time when the computer industry that Ault served was going through a painful period of slow sales and declining margins.

"Ault had already filed application papers with their bank and received verbal assurances of approval, when the company received some bad news: one of its largest clients had just filed for bankruptcy. With this new information, the bank no longer had current and accurate information. The critical issue was that with this impending bankruptcy, Ault might not receive the large sum owed to it by the customer or a continuing stream of cash flow. Over 30 percent of the projected annual revenues shown on the forecasted profit-and-loss statement were no longer accurate."

Lucy cut in, "That's like being between a rock and a hard place!" Pete agreed, understanding the grave implications of the situation.

"The Ault executives," Kip continued, "faced a dilemma, just like the people at Coleman had. If they shared this latest information with the bank and revised their financials,

151

the company's position would not look nearly so strong, and they would almost certainly be denied the increase to the line of credit.

"Without these new funds the company would have to lay off 20 percent of its valued employees. And that's not all. Ault executives were anticipating the computer economy would be strengthened early the next year. Without the employees, the company would be less competitive."

"I understand—boy, do I understand!" said Pete.

"At the same time, Ault's leaders were confident that news about the bankruptcy would almost certainly not come to the bank's attention for months. And it wasn't even a question of lying; they could simply play dumb, wait until the line of credit had been increased and the funds committed, and then let the bank know of the changed situation.

"The good of the company seemed to demand playing it this way. Who would ever know? Despite the strong temptation, Ault's executives had embraced the freedom-based philosophy, which is steeped in a Shared Values ethic, and they knew from the beginning that their corporate values required telling the truth, not only when it was convenient but in all situations."

"So what happened?" asked Yolanda.

"The bank's reaction was not what the company expected or feared," replied Kip. "One Ault official later said to me that by taking the risk of sharing the information with the bank and telling the truth immediately, they had gained the bank's respect. Indeed, the bankers were so deeply impressed by the company's straightforward truthfulness that the relationship was strengthened." Kip smiled at his table-mates.

"So it was a good-news story for a freedom-based workplace, wasn't it?" stated Pete.

"Yes, Pete, it was," responded Kip.

"Kip, what were Ault's Shared Values, and would these be the same Shared Values that every organization should embrace if they want a freedom-based workplace?" asked Lucy.

"Yes, Lucy, they are," replied Kip.

"These eight Shared Values are the same ones that Ault and every company I work with embraces to create freedom-based conditions."

Having said that, Kip handed Lucy a piece of paper on which the eight Shared Values were printed.

"And remember, too, that these eight Shared Values are the key values to connecting people to their jobs. If you want accountability to flourish, you have to practice these eight strategies every day. Like the broken windows theory, if you ignore any one of these elements, antisocial behavior will occur. Why? Because silence on any one of these implies tacit support that it's OK to break the rules.

If you want to create the conditions for accountability to flourish, you have to practice these eight strategies every day. Like the broken windows theory, if you ignore any one of these elements, antisocial behavior will occur.

"These eight values were identified by seventeen million people from forty countries responding to surveys. Let me illustrate them for you using Ault's experience as my example."

Getting a paper napkin from the waiter, Kip took the time before explaining each of the eight Shared Values to write it on the napkin. "OK," he said, "the first principle of Shared Values is 'Treat others with uncompromising truth.'

"Despite not wanting to disclose the bankruptcy of one of their biggest customers," he said, "Ault's leadership team decided that the right thing to do was to disclose this fact to their bank, immediately. While doing so might have cost them the loan they were counting on, they preferred to disclose the uncompromising truth anyway. As it turned out, their bankers were impressed with their truthfulness and made the loan."

Again, Kip stopped his explanation to write on the napkin: "Lavish trust on your associates."

"While most organizations would consider their bank an interchangeable vendor, Ault's leadership team lavished trust on their bankers and treated them as partners. By reporting what they had learned about their bankrupt customer as soon as they became aware of the news, Ault's leaders strengthened the trust their bankers had in them.

Kip wrote, "Mentor unselfishly," while saying, "It certainly was tempting to keep their mouths shut until after their loan had been approved. In fact, this course of action was seriously discussed. But when it came time to make a decision, the CEO mentored his people to stick to their Shared Values, which included being unselfish in offering full disclosure.

Continuing, Kip wrote, "Be receptive to new ideas, regardless of their origin."

"After all, 'Business is business' had once been their motto, but after they'd adopted Shared Values, their point of view changed completely. Even though there was the potentially negative impact of being denied the much-needed line of credit, members of the leadership team were receptive to new ideas regardless of their origin.

"'Take personal risks for the organization's sake,'" Kip said as he wrote. "Choosing to disclose the information was more than an ethical dilemma; it meant taking a personal risk for every member of the company. Their livelihoods were on the line! But, more important, so was their integrity. In the end, they chose to risk the possibility of a short-term loss of income over a long-term loss of their reputations and the loyalty of their employees and the community. Here is an example of a publicly traded company that took their integrity seriously and by doing so protected their stockholders. During those years, in the mid-1990s when I was working with Ault, their stock rose by over 1,000 percent."

"Kip, it sounds like shareholder integrity won out over shareholder value, and it paid off, too!" said Lucy with admiration.

Kip smiled at Lucy as he wrote, "'Give credit where it is due.'"

"Lucy," he said, "part of giving credit is giving timely and appropriate feedback when our actions are not up to our individual or group standards. Since their standards called for uncompromising truth, no one on the management team was willing to take credit for withholding the truth. Rather, they were prepared to give credit where it was due for sticking to their values.

"Number 7 is 'Do not touch dishonest dollars,'" Kip said as he wrote. "The people of Ault manufacturing had clearly defined their standards of honesty, and those standards were nonnegotiable. Together Ault employees understood the organization's Shared Values and Keen Internal Vision. Everyone was prepared to support the values they shared. One of their values was to never touch a dishonest dollar. Maintaining their collective honesty and integrity was of far greater value than any amount of money or protecting their stock price."

Kip wrote, "Put the interests of others before your own," and said, "The final decision to tell the bank about their customer's bankruptcy came down to one simple question: Were they prepared to put the interests of the bank before their own? The answer was a resounding *yes!* The good people of Ault had learned from experience that putting the interests of others first was the only way to build a healthy relationship with their bankers and with their customers.

"Yolanda, Lucy, and Pete, do these Shared Values make sense to you?" asked Kip.

"They make a lot of sense, Kip," answered Pete. "I've got to believe they would make sense to anyone."

"Yes, Kip, I wish I had them at my incentive company," said Yolanda.

Laughing, Lucy chimed in, "Boy, would this make a difference with our partners. The competitiveness and withholding of information in my organization are incredible," she said, shaking her head.

Within a few moments of Lucy's comments, the waiter and an assistant appeared with the group's main courses and cleared away their salad plates.

Pete looked at the group. "I think we should all give this a rest for the moment and not let our food get cold." They all agreed and began their dinner as the conversation turned lightheartedly to family and trivial banter.

What had started off as a contentious discussion between strangers had become a constructive meeting of minds.

12

Taking Personal Responsibility Is a Challenge for Everyone!

Anxious to continue their earlier topic, Pete noticed that the group was almost finished eating and said, "OK, maybe it's time to get back to business." The group laughed as they looked up from their plates.

"Kip," continued Pete, "we've talked about establishing the right conditions and about Shared Values. Is there anything more we need to do to create the right conditions to increase the chances of improving the accountability of our people?"

Kip finished chewing the last bite of his meal and looked at Pete. "Yes, there is," he said, "and it has to do with getting everyone to be responsible for their actions and behaviors. In order for all people to become accountable, traditional roles must change."

"What do you mean, 'traditional roles must change?'" asked Yolanda.

"Let me see if I can explain," broke in Pete. "Kip's given me a little more insight into this aspect of the freedom-based philosophy, so let's see if I've learned anything today." Pete smiled at Kip, and Kip was most pleased to let Pete carry the freedom-based flag.

Pete said, "People at every level must be allowed to assume responsibility for tasks that in control-based management systems have traditionally been reserved for managers."

Lucy was very interested in this aspect of the freedom-based approach and jumped in, saying, "You know, that may be one of the missing elements that I was talking about earlier. I've observed that when our organization comes into a company with our systems, it's as though the staff becomes even more passive, and *that's* where the breakdown occurs. What we begin seeing exhibited is passive-aggressive behavior instead of volunteerism and proactive actions."

While Kip nodded his head in agreement, Yolanda said, "I think Lucy makes a good point. We see similar behaviors when we throw a really big incentive program into a company. Sure, some of the people get excited, but others glaze over."

Pete waited until Yolanda finished her comment and then continued. "Kip suggested that learning to share these responsibilities requires time, patience, and practice as all staff members adjust to their new roles. Now I'm stuck, Kip, so I'm turning this over to you for more embellishment," said Pete with respect.

"You did a great job," said Kip, pausing. "Let me see if I can add one or two things about how we get everyone to jump on board. I think the best way to explain how you accomplish this is by giving you an example. Please remember, in the old days, only managers were allowed to be responsible. Now that may seem silly, but it really isn't."

"I don't think that's silly," said Yolanda. "My dad worked for General Motors for over thirty years and retired in the late seventies. He was a shop foreman, and he used to tell the story of an incident that supports your comment. Let me see if I can remember it." She reflected a moment and then said, "OK, in 1971, the union started to place posters in the assembly areas so the workers could read them. One of the posters was particularly disturbing to management."

"What did it say?" asked Pete.

"Well, it was really pretty nondescript," said Yolanda, "at least that's what the workers thought, but management really got angry and called in the union foreman, my dad, and demanded that he take down the poster."

"So, what did it say?" asked Pete again.

"It said, 'Quality is everyone's job!'" said Yolanda.

"Why would anyone get angry about that?" asked Lucy.

"Well, as my dad tells the story, management felt that quality was *their* job and only their job. And that it was the role of labor to do what management directed," said Yolanda.

"Imagine the stupidity of that," said Pete in disgust. "No wonder we got our brains kicked in by foreign competitors," he said, shaking his head.

"Pete, don't be so hard on these managers," said Kip. "Remember the context of the situation. There are many examples of how American industry has changed since then."

"Yes, they have—but we have one long way to go!" exclaimed Lucy.

"The key is that now we have a chance to invite workers at every level to become responsible," pointed out Kip, "responsible to own their jobs and to come up with creative solutions. But before they'll be able to do all the activities of the manager of old, we have to allow the staff time to embrace skills that will support their new roles in an operation's everyday activities. And we need to retool the managers' skills to fit leaders instead of managers, mentors instead of directors, and teachers instead of dictators. The key transitional concept is that we want staff members to drive all the processes, systems, and job functions, and we want the old managers to transform into resources."

Lucy began to understand where Kip was going with his explanation and strategy.

"Kip, you call these new leaders Wise Counsels, don't you?" said Pete.

"Yes, Pete, that's the term—Wise Counsels," reiterated Kip.

The two ladies recognized that Kip had taken on the role of their Wise Counsel.

Lucy wondered aloud, "OK, so how do I become a Wise Counsel?"

"We've found a very elegant approach for starting this transformation, for both labor and management," said Kip.

"First, let me tell you our goal. Our goal is to teach all staff members how to study issues, how to experiment with possible solutions, and how to take on new responsibilities. And our goal at the supervisory level is to transform them into leaders who act as resources, not task-oriented managers. To accomplish this, we ask leaders to hand over responsibility for the completion of tasks to their people. We use a project approach, using a task force to teach these skills to staff and leadership."

"This kind of sounds like my experience in officer candidate school when we would go on warfare maneuvers where they'd use live ammunition to simulate a real battle," said Pete.

"Yes, Pete, there's no replacing live ammo zooming over his or her head to get the attention of a soldier in training," said the older man, smiling.

"Here's how we do it," continued Kip. "The best way to explain the approach is to tell you about another organization I worked with, a small beer distributor in northern California. After the organization had adopted the eight Shared Values, we split their employees into task forces, each group studying a different business issue. Imagine, every employee being involved in the process of learning to take on new responsibilities!"

Kip handed a copy of the learning objectives of a task force experience to Lucy. As she was looking over the learning objectives, she took note of how excited Kip had become about this issue.

Staff Goal: To teach all staff members how to study issues, how to experiment with possible solutions, and how to take on new responsibilities

Leadership Goal: To transform old-style, take-charge managers into leaders who act as resources, not managers

To Accomplish This: We ask the leadership to hand over the responsibility for the completion of the task to their people.

The Vehicle We Use: A project approach, using a task force to teach new skills to staff and leaders

Kip continued, more animated than before. "At the conclusion of their task force, each group wrote a White Paper summarizing the information that they'd gathered and the problems they'd identified. In large operations of several thousand, hundreds of these papers are generated, reviewed, and published for everyone to see. Talk about change from a control-based environment!"

He reflected on what a remarkable transformation this approach had had on the rank-and-file worker. "Twenty year truck drivers had never been asked their opinion on anything. Now they were being asked to analyze and develop comprehensive strategies, something they would never have been involved in before.

"Picture this scenario if you will: Joe, who's driven a truck for two decades, comes home to his wife and family a different man after his first task force meeting.

"His wife asks, 'How was work?' In the old days, Joe would've grunted because driving a truck and delivering beer was all he'd known."

"That's enough to make anyone grunt," said Lucy, laughing.

Kip smiled. "But now, Joe comes home and starts talking about his task force meeting where a new advertising campaign is being planned with four-color collateral material for a point-of-sale display."

"Talk about a head snap," said Yolanda. "Joe's wife must've thought her husband had been abducted by aliens!"

"Or sampled too much of the product!" said Pete, laughing.

Everyone laughed, but they also knew that Kip was telling a story that they found fascinating. The radical nature of this approach was significant, and each one of Kip's colleagues could appreciate how this task force experience would forever change Joe and the entire operation. After this experience there would be no going back to a control-based workplace where men and women were used as beasts of burden and asked to leave their brains at the company's front door.

"OK," Kip continued, "now you understand the fundamental goal of this approach, so let's get more specific.

"One of the task forces studied the company's point-of-sale (POS) process. They used POS material in their retail establishments to attract the attention of the consumer and to create greater brand awareness. Their POS included items such as price cards, posters, cardboard displays, and the like.

"There were a number of issues the task force wanted to study, such as how POS material was ordered, received, stored, distributed, and tracked. And for their retail accounts, of course, they wanted to find out which POS items were most effective on their customers.

"The task force leaders started by asking all members to assist in the process of gathering information for the POS study. Some of the task force members were reluctant to participate at first. But after a few meetings, most were fully involved."

Yolanda asked, "Are you talking about people like Joe, the truck driver?"

"I sure am, Yolanda," answered Kip. "As they gathered information, people on the task force began to get a clearer picture of the real issues and problems inherent with POS. From the information gathered, they were able to determine a number of issues, which they prioritized." Kip began ticking off examples from the issues that surfaced:

1. There is no set budget for annual POS purchases.

2. The master schedule for themed POS, like Christmas, St. Patrick's Day, and the Superbowl, is not working well.

3. There is no set staging area for receiving POS.

4. The POS storage area is dirty, disorganized, and poorly lighted.

5. There is a great deal of wasted POS that's literally thrown into the trash.

6. There is no POS orientation procedure for those who handle the material.

"In addition, the salespeople who used the POS had developed the habit of hoarding it so that they would have enough POS when they needed it. Despite hoarding, much of the POS was thrown out without ever being used. It was clear that any proposed solution would have to deal with these issues in a proactive way.

"Energy and enthusiasm began to flow as individual task force members became comfortable with stepping forward with their own creative ideas. At the same time, the task force leader began to move away from the table, allowing the task force members to share leadership and to take on greater levels of responsibility."

"What do you mean, he moved away from the table?" asked Yolanda.

"Yolanda, the task force leader literally moved his chair to the corner of the room. He became a resource to the group," explained Kip.

"Are you telling us the manager abandoned the group in the middle of the project?" asked Lucy.

"That's a great question," acknowledged Kip. "Lucy—"

Pete interrupted by asking, "Kip, can I address Lucy on her point?" Kip made a sweeping motion with his hand to indicate to Pete that he was only too happy to have him take over.

"Here's how I would explain it," said Pete. "The task force leader's purpose, or goal, is to become a Wise Counsel, a resource to the group—right, Kip? The key is that you want the group leader to become an adviser and not the primary driver of the task force. That's the big strategy in transitioning the decision-making power or responsibility to the task force members."

Pete looked at Kip with deep respect and continued. "You know, the idea is a brilliant metaphor: *Move away from the table without abandoning the group.* And he didn't appoint anyone to take his place but encouraged shared leadership."

"You're exactly right," Kip said, as he continued without missing a beat. "As the task force members began to organize their ideas, the outline for what eventually became their

White Paper began to emerge. The task force, with the mentoring of its leader, developed new policies and processes for ordering, inventorying, distributing, and placing POS.

Move away from the table without abandoning the group.

Yolanda said dumbfoundedly, "And we're still talking about truck drivers and administrative people who in the old days would never have been invited into these kinds of meetings!"

Kip went on: "That's right, Yolanda. The new approach to who leads puts the responsibility for the whole process in the hands of the salespeople who are responsible for ordering, storing, and placing POS in their own sales territories—not in management's hands. Each salesperson is also responsible for developing and monitoring his or her own POS budget. By crafting their transformation, managers became Wise Counsels.

"Although several model POS systems were available from their distributors nationally, Joe's company developed a new system that fit the unique needs of their own local organization.

"Let me give you an overview of the new responsibilities the task force took on during the course of developing their White Paper." Kip began ticking off the keys to developing responsibility at every level and related each one to the task force's development:

"Number 1 is *planning*: All task force members took an active role in gathering information and strategizing future actions in an organized manner. Task force members shared responsibility for planning the task force meetings and for deciding who would gather the needed information.

"Number 2 is *priority setting*: Setting priorities became possible when everyone on the task force understood the big picture. Task force members began to see how the current system worked and how much was budgeted for POS annually. They also identified and prioritized problems with the current system that needed to be addressed.

"Three is *removing roadblocks*: The task force members took on the challenge of figuring out how to remove the road-blocks to an efficient and effective POS system. They uncovered and removed all the red tape, all the turf-building behaviors, and all the hidden agendas inherent in the existing system. Rigid POS policies and procedures were replaced with policies that would allow individuals to gladly accept personal responsibility.

"Four is *creativity*: The task force worked hard at fostering a can-do attitude, one where inspiration, energy, enthusiasm, fun, loyalty, personal engagement, and commitment to one another became the springboards to creative ideas. They understood that without creativity, the task force's vitality would quickly vanish.

"Number 5 is *task completion*: Everyone on the task force understood the importance of allowing individual salespeople the right to manage their own POS without the sales manager monitoring their activity or swooping in to take over the process again. Task force members were provided with open access to the information they needed, and they gained a sense of pride and enhanced self-esteem as they completed the White Paper together.

"Six is *risk taking*: Task force members learned how to take appropriate risks—that is, risks proportionate to the potential benefits to the organization. Rather than abandoning all controls, which might lead to anarchy, the task force developed flexible policies and processes that would enable each individual involved in handling POS to take appropriate creative risks. They anticipated mistakes in judgment due to lack of experience. However, with practice and experience using the new policies and processes, risk taking became a welcomed activity, supported by Wise Counsels who provided resources when asked.

"The seventh is *policy setting*: The POS policies became very localized; that is, the people responsible for owning the new POS system became responsible for setting the new policies and accountable to each other for staying on budget. Their motto became 'Those that own the game create the rules.' POS policies were transformed from rigid controls to flexible support systems.

"Eight is *self-expression*: The task force members learned to make the new POS system an expression of themselves, uniquely designed to fit the needs of their own organization. Believing that there is no one best way of doing things, they remain prepared to modify the system in the future so that the POS policy will continue to meet their needs."

"Under the new system, the sales supervisors are no longer accountable for the process, and so they no longer monitor the activities. This is an important point, so let me restate this. The salespeople, not the supervisors, are accountable for the entire process!"

"Kip," remarked Pete incredulously, "in the old days, only guys from the home office would have been allowed to touch this subject!"

"That's right, Pete," Kip said, "not in a thousand years would this have happened before the organization's transformation."

The salespeople, not the supervisors, are accountable for the entire process!

"One important measure of success," Kip continued, "was a reduction of waste. By implementing the new system, they were able to reduce waste by over 30 percent!"

"Now that's bottom-line results!" said Lucy, punctuating her remark with her fork.

Kip smiled. "That's not all! They also achieved several other important results:

Task Force Accomplishments

1. Established a system for receiving and storing POS

2. Set up a clean, well-organized, well-lighted storage area

3. Developed a POS orientation for new employees

4. Set up a semiannual POS budgeting process that directly involved each salesperson

5. Created a master schedule for themed POS

6. Eliminated hoarding

7. Helped improve sales by getting the right kinds of POS into each account

8. Reduced waste by 30 percent."

"That's all unbelievable!" said Yolanda.

The group nodded in concurrence, as Lucy said, "Kip, let me take a crack at the net-net of what you've told us while you finish your pie."

Lucy began, and everyone once again could see why she was such an effective consultant. She was a quick learner and spoke well off the cuff. "Organizations begin the process of transformation to a freedom-based work environment," reasoned Lucy, "by creating the right conditions for extraordinary performance. They do this by emphasizing Shared Values and by teaching a new approach to taking responsibility. This means that the context and roles must change."

As Lucy finished expounding on these concepts and the outcome of the task force example Kip had shared with the group, Kip knew that his colleagues were getting the message and personally taking to heart these new ideas. He now recognized that Lucy, Yolanda, and Pete would eventually spread the news that a new way of treating people and reaching higher levels of performance and service was possible.

13

Transformation Begins with a Visionary Leader

The group was enjoying their dessert when Pete asked Kip another clarifying question. "Kip, earlier today you very briefly mentioned the Visionary Leader, and you've spoken exclusively about the Wise Counsel. What's the difference?"

Kip took a moment to finish his last bite of pie and turned to Pete while the ladies talked between themselves. "I'd be glad to explain, Pete. As I mentioned earlier, a Wise Counsel uses three primary strategies. First, they share a Keen Internal Vision at every opportunity."

Pete chimed in, "Teachable moments!"

"Right," nodded Kip. "Second, Wise Counsels become resources to people, and, third, they wait to be asked. What I mean by that is, they will not take ownership for a staff member's or team's job. If they did, they'd be taking accountability away from that very person or group."

"OK, so that's a summary of the Wise Counsel's role, but what about the role of the Visionary Leader?" asked Pete. At this point Yolanda and Lucy began to pick up on the two men's discussion.

"The Visionary Leader uses all these strategies," Kip explained, "but in addition offers the organization much more.

But, first, let me tell you all a little more about the Wise Counsel and who can become a Wise Counsel before we delve into the Visionary Leader's role." He realized that the ladies had become interested in the subject, and since the role of the Wise Counsel to sustain a workplace that supports accountability is crucial, he felt it should not be underestimated or overlooked.

Kip reflected a moment and then began. "Since being a Wise Counsel is one of the most highly valued roles in a freedom-based operation, there is opportunity for every staff member to be a Wise Counsel. This is not a role reserved for persons in positions of authority but is available to any person who selflessly shares his or her knowledge and skills with others. Since all members of the organization can be Wise Counsels, leadership is shared and strengthened across the entire organization, from the very top to the very bottom."

"Could you give me an example of what you mean?" asked Lucy, getting more involved with the explanation.

"Of course," said Kip. "Not too long ago, a worker on the production line of one of the largest glass fabrication firms in the United States got into a heated dispute with his lead. The worker had rejected a finished product, and the lead, a new man in that position, was insisting the problem was minor and the product should be released for shipping." Kip looked at Yolanda, Lucy, and Pete, each in turn, as he spoke. "This organization was still making the transition to a freedom-based operation, and I was working closely with them.

"The glass product itself was perfect; the only defect lay with the company's own colorful logo, which had become stretched and distorted while it was being applied.

"The worker was unwilling to let the product go out the door with a less-than-perfect company logo, while the lead, answerable for production rates and completing work on schedule, insisted, 'We're not selling the logo—the product is good and it goes.' Remember, the complete transformation to a freedom-based workplace had not taken place yet. Some of the aspects were in place, but not the most essential one."

"And that would be what?" asked Yolanda.

"The most essential element, Yolanda, is simply who is accountable for production, quality, and meeting shipping schedules," responded Kip. "At this juncture it was still the lead who was ultimately accountable, not the production worker."

"Boy, this story's sounding familiar—slam it out no matter what," said Pete with a grimace.

Kip nodded and continued with this real-life story. "The shift supervisor was called in to mediate and listened to each man explain his position. As a Wise Counsel, he knew that he would have to find a way of guiding these two men toward reaching an understanding, a way of maintaining respect for one another, and a way of allowing each man to maintain his dignity. But this was an ownership issue as well as a quality issue."

"So what happened?" asked Yolanda.

"Asking the lead to join him out of everyone else's hearing range, the shift supervisor carefully explained the importance of the logo. 'Logos are very important,' he pointed out. 'Major companies spend millions on their design. Receiving product with a defective logo is like picking up a new car from the dealer and discovering it has a dent; the car runs just as well, it's just as comfortable, gets just as good mileage—but it's not perfect.'

"The lead understood the shift supervisor's point but countered, 'We'll take a hit to our production rate if the product doesn't ship.' The shift supervisor, again acting as Wise Counsel, replied, 'It's been my experience that good production rates will come when everyone on the line takes them seriously.' And he went on. 'Because as a lead you're on display every minute of the day, how you deal with a situation like this is very important. If you override the production worker's decision, you might damage the morale and performance of the whole line, and, most important of all, you're taking responsibility for something that we want the frontline worker to own. And that may be the most important issue facing us—who ultimately owns the work.'

"The shift supervisor acknowledged the lead's motivation of wanting to do his best to keep production levels high. He and the lead also talked about why the worker was upset and how the lead might handle the situation without losing face.

"The supervisor later reported that his greatest satisfaction from the whole experience was in seeing how the lead learned a lesson about allowing his people to be accountable for their own decisions." Kip looked around for comments from the group.

"OK, this is a good example of the right kind of coaching," acknowledged Yolanda, "and I see the differentiation between traditional coaching and the Wise Counsel approach. But how efficient is this approach?" asked Yolanda.

"That's a great question," responded Kip, "and an important one for the entire operation. Whereas managers, according to actual time studies, spend upward of 75 percent of their time on activities like scheduling, directing activity, generating production reports, managing inventory, and troubleshooting in a traditional control-based enterprise, in contrast, Wise Counsels expect staff members and work groups to manage these activities themselves. This frees a Wise Counsel to spend the bulk of his or her time coaching, mentoring, and being a resource."

"Kip, is it really possible to spend the bulk of your time coaching, mentoring, and being a resource?" asked Lucy, with a skeptical tone. Pete was also interested in Kip's answer.

"Lucy, not in a control-based management system," replied Kip. "But in a freedom-based work environment, it happens every day, and it's estimated by some sources that in control-based organizations, managers struggle to spend 10 percent of their time coaching and mentoring. There are so many things competing for their time and attention: reports to write, meetings to attend, and, of course, people who need to be managed."

Pete broke in. "My own experience suggests that the actual time spent mentoring and coaching in most organizations is significantly less than 10 percent. Certainly that's what our outside consultants told us, and it was one of our greatest challenges as we tried to initiate quality programs throughout our operations."

Kip added, "However, in a freedom-based organization, because staff members have taken on most of the responsibilities previously reserved for managers, Wise Counsels are routinely able to spend up to 60 percent of their time mentoring and coaching."

Control-Based Workplace— 10 Percent Coaching and Mentoring

Freedom-Based Environment— 60 Percent Coaching and Mentoring

"You're implying that the frontline workers should produce production reports and manage inventory," countered Lucy with some skepticism, adding, "If the workers are doing all that, who's getting the work done?" Yolanda laughed.

Kip responded good-naturedly. "I know it's hard to believe, but when workers are managing themselves, doing their own planning and reporting, they're significantly more productive than they were when the boss was handling those chores."

"Let me guess the reason," said Pete. "The reason they're so much more efficient is that they waste far less time waiting for orders, inspections, and approvals, and, more important, they're able to make adjustments on the fly without having to check with anyone because they have a Keen Internal Vision guiding them."

"Let me take a crack, also," said Lucy, cutting off both Pete and Kip and jumping into the fray. "The Wise Counsels set the stage for greater productivity by modeling Shared Values behavior, don't they?"

Kip nodded in respect for his colleagues' insights. "You're both right on! When staff members ask for advice on decisions, often the first question asked by a Wise Counsel is, 'What do our values say about this decision?' In this way, values are used as the primary filter for everyday decision making."

"You know, I think that idea would work wonders in my plants," said Pete enthusiastically. "Frankly, we can't supervise fast enough."

"Yes, but will your workers voluntarily take the risks associated with this new approach?" said Yolanda.

Kip smiled. "Another great question, Yolanda," he noted, in a congratulatory tone. "There are already plenty of risks when a decision has to be made. The real question is, who is best qualified to make the decision? We'd answer, it's the person on the frontline who is best qualified."

"And that makes perfect sense *if* the person has the big picture," said Lucy.

Kip nodded. "A Wise Counsel, by virtue of his or her knowledge and experience, has frequent opportunities to coach and mentor staff members so they get that big picture, as you call it," said Kip. "That's why a Wise Counsel needs the full 60 percent of his or her time to make the big pictures clear and make sure the staff is comfortable enough to take the associated risks.

"And believe it or not," said Kip, turning to Yolanda, "people who understand the big picture don't need any external incentives to be fully engaged—and that's the beauty of intrinsic motivation."

Yolanda understood Kip's point and appreciated the clarity of the example. She was now open to an alternative idea. She now knew what would eventually take the place of the incentive business: the new business would be based on building a freedom-based environment with a foundation of intrinsic motivation as the reward system. Smiling to herself, Yolanda recognized an enormous business opportunity.

Pete took his turn in the dialogue. "However, much of what passes for coaching in a control-based environment is, in fact, judging, isn't it?"

"Yes," said Kip. "Discussing a staff member's weaknesses or telling him or her what *not* to do is both ineffective and demoralizing, and it distracts the person from the big picture. Often when a person is criticized, he or she stops listening and taking risks. Good coaches master the ability to give information that is easily understood and immediately useable."

Discussing a staff member's weaknesses or telling him or her what not to do is both ineffective and demoralizing, and it distracts the person from the big picture. Good coaches master the ability to give information that is easily understood and immediately useable.

"Tell me more about this coaching technique," asked Lucy.

"My pleasure," said Kip. "By using simple and nonjudgmental observations, such as 'Do a little more of this and a little less of that,' people get information they can use. This more-and-less style of coaching is effective because it's understandable, it's easy to accept because it's nonjudgmental, and it's immediately applicable. And the best part is that coaches don't need much training, and everyone seems to get the technique almost immediately. It goes like this: 'Lucy, I need more listening and less talking.' That's it; it's that simple. Just tell them what you suggest they change."

The best part is that you don't need much training, and everyone seems to get the technique almost immediately. Just tell them what you suggest they change.

Kip finished his point: "Whether coaching involves on-the-job mentoring or classroom training, the role of a Wise Counsel is to be sure that coaching is available to staff members when they most need it."

"I like your more-and-less coaching model," said Pete. "As I think about it, some of my best coaches were Wise Counsels. But, Kip, you still haven't touched on the role of the Visionary Leader."

Kip paused to take a sip of water and continued. "Let me see if I can be very specific on this subject. It's starting to get late, and I don't know about all you young folks, but I'm getting tired. So here goes.

"First and foremost, a Visionary Leader is motivated to serve, *not* rule. Some have called it 'servant leadership.'[1]

"Without getting overly complicated, I believe there are four gifts that leaders provide: authorship, love, power, and significance.[2] With the gift of authorship, a leader allows people to develop their skills and accomplish something of lasting value. By giving love, a leader shows people he or she cares enough to find out what really matters. Giving the gift of power allows people to tap into their own talents and intellect to find answers. And the fourth gift, the gift of significance, helps people understand that they can be part of making the world better."[3]

Lucy responded thoughtfully, "I really like what you just said."

Kip chuckled. "Let's not get serious on me now, Lucy. Please understand that the Visionary Leader starts with self-awareness and self-acceptance, and he or she doesn't walk on water. They are works in progress, aware of their incompleteness and flaws. At the same time, they accept that the gifts they possess are adequate for the task of leadership. They use their talent, intellect, authority, and access to resources to serve people and to make the organization's Keen Internal Vision a reality for everyone."

"I'd imagine that every staff member needs to understand how he or she contributes to that vision," said Pete.

"Visionary Leaders also let the community know how the organization is progressing toward the vision," Kip continued. "Sometimes this calls for a Visionary Leader to lead in celebration. At other times, it means delivering bad news and then rallying the staff members to the new challenge. Sometimes it means asking for extraordinary sacrifices when the survival of the organization is at stake."

"Kip, what do you think is the toughest part of being a Visionary Leader?" asked Yolanda.

"Perhaps the toughest part of being a Visionary Leader is learning to let go," Kip pointed out. "While the popular image of a leader is one who takes charge, a freedom-based Visionary Leader knows that flexibility and openness are much more powerful. Visionary Leaders understand, accept, and apply the concept of noncontrol.[4] Rather than exerting power through rigid controls to achieve the organization's Keen Internal Vision, a Visionary Leader trusts his or her people to achieve the vision."

"Being a Visionary Leader sounds like no small task," commented Pete. "From your description, they are self-aware, flexible, and open. They are motivated to serve others and to bring people together around a common vision. They lead the celebrations and are willing to share bad news when necessary, even when the bad news is financial."

Lucy interrupted with one of her cute comments. "Yeah, and they leap tall buildings in a single bound!"

Kip chuckled and then apologized for bringing everyone back on track. "Just one more important point, if you'd allow me. Every organization, even freedom-based organizations, needs to focus on cash flow and profit. Without cash flow, salaries cannot be paid or operating expenses met. Without profit, funds are not available for routine maintenance, for capital expenditures, or for investments in the future. Even nonprofit organizations need cash flow and profit. And the way a freedom-based operation handles this crucial point is to keep everyone involved in the P&L of the business. There are lots of different approaches to involving staff in the financial business of the enterprise. But it's getting late, and suffice to say, that without people knowing what's going on, they can't be financial stewards of the business, and the business will fail."[5]

Pete broke in, with some amusement. "The recent dot-com crash bears testimony to this immutable law." The others nodded in agreement at this observation.

"Kip, before we call it a night, I have one other question. What's the single best indicator of financial health?" asked Lucy.

"I've found employee satisfaction to be the leading indicator for present and future financial health—bar none!" said Kip. "It's even more important than monitoring productivity, turnover, employee accidents, or injury rates, because these numbers are the outcome of the level of employee satisfaction."

"Interesting," said Lucy. "So these other indicators are symptoms of a workforce in turmoil, not the cause?"

"Absolutely," said Kip decisively. "Independent studies have shown a direct link between employee satisfaction and the bottom line, and my experience using the Values & Attitude Study confirms it."[6]

Kip and Pete noticed that they were once again the only guests still in the dining car. Pete said, "I think we're starting to make a habit of closing the place down." The others laughed.

Yolanda added, "I'm calling it a night." The others agreed. As a last parting shot, Lucy called out to Yolanda, "Say good night to Hank for us!" Kip looked at Pete and shook his head.

14

The Freedom-Based Philosophy Is Adopted One Person at a Time

By the time Pete awoke the next morning, Kip had already risen. The blankets on his berth were pulled up over his pillow and his suitcase rested on them. Pete shaved and dressed and walked briskly down to the dining car where he found Kip and Lucy seated alone, reading the newspaper and drinking coffee.

"Good morning, Lucy, Kip," said Pete.

"Hello, yourself," said Lucy.

"Good morning," said Kip.

"Gosh, it's nearly eight o'clock. I don't know when I last slept so long or so well," said Pete.

"That's one of the nice things about train travel," said Kip smiling. "You can really relax. Would you like some coffee? I know they're still serving breakfast if you'd like to order."

After Pete had ordered breakfast, he said, "You know, Kip, I've been thinking: How do you go about spreading the freedom-based philosophy across the whole organization? Do the managers teach this, or does someone else?"

Lucy put her newspaper down. "I'd like to know about that, too."

Kip answered, "Pete and Lucy, as you can imagine, there's a role for every member of an organization in implementing a freedom-based workplace, but there are four types of people who are particularly helpful in spreading the freedom-based philosophy."

"Hi, everyone. Have you seen Striker?" Yolanda's eyes were darting around the dining car. "He said he wanted to have breakfast with me, and there's nowhere to hide." Everyone laughed.

Lucy said, "Kip was beginning to tell us how to spread the freedom-based philosophy throughout an operation. Here, scoot in on my side of the table; now your buddy Hank won't have room to join us." Yolanda did as she was told, and the foursome again became focused on creating a freedom-based workplace.

"Excuse me for interrupting," apologized Yolanda. "Please go on."

"The winning strategy," began Kip, "is to identify and employ the assistance of four special types of people to create your freedom-based workplace. It's important also to note that you need not engage all of your people at once. But with the help of these four extraordinary types of people within any organization, you can successfully begin the transformation."

"So I don't have to put everyone in my company in one of the four categories. Whew, that's a relief," said Pete.

"Pete, I got this idea from Malcolm Gladwell. He describes it as the 'The Law of the Few.' In his Law of the Few, Gladwell identifies three types of people necessary to ignite social change. He calls the first type Mavens—I call them Collectors, we both call the second type Connectors, and he calls the third type Salesmen—I call them Persuaders.[1] You might want to pick up Malcolm Gladwell's book for the clarity of his descriptions and the help his ideas could be to you and many of your senior people.

"To his list, I've added a fourth type I believe to be essential for organizational change."

Pete broke in: "It's Visionary Leaders, isn't it?"

"Yes, Pete, it is," Kip said. "Let me give you a brief summary of each key role.

"First, let's talk about the Collectors. Collectors enjoy exploring new ways of doing things and sharing what they've learned with others. Collectors are the members of your organization who are excited about new ideas and love to share them with their coworkers. They are usually the first folks to get excited about a new idea like a freedom-based environment.

> *Collectors enjoy exploring new ways of doing things and sharing what they have learned with others.*

"Collectors are exceptionally receptive to new ideas of all kinds. In fact, when I work with an operation, I always ask for a small group of middle managers that possesses the natural tendency of being Collectors to help us spread the word.

"Collectors don't just passively collect and share new ideas. They are sincerely interested in helping people put new ideas to work. Others in the organization recognize that a collector's motivation is not in any way selfish, which is a very effective way of getting people to pay attention to the new ideas he or she brings. Collectors have both the knowledge and the social skills to spread new ideas."

"I think I know exactly the type of person you're describing," said Pete excitedly. "I get clippings from one of them every week. Some of our best teachers are by your definition Collectors. And I've observed many of our Collectors love being students and frequently ask us to send them to learn something new."

"Yeah, I work with some of those guys in our consulting division," interjected Lucy. "Those are the guys who twenty years ago sneaked desktop computers into the office under their raincoats."

Everyone laughed.

"I hope they had more than a computer under their raincoats," said Yolanda mischievously. Pete seemed somewhat embarrassed by the last joke, but Kip was having a ball.

Pete continued trying to get back to business. "Come to think of it, the wife of one of my best friend's is a Collector. She's an elementary school teacher, but her talent is collecting ideas. To begin with, she reads voraciously. Charged with teaching third and fourth graders at her school, she provides her students with hundreds of books from which to choose.

"I asked her why she has so many books in her room, and she told me that kids develop reading skills at different rates. The books in her room range from first- through eighth-grade reading levels.

"She's passionate about reading and is determined to spread her passion to her students. She has even helped develop an innovative new reading program, and the results have been sensational. Whereas in most classrooms, kids groan at the prospect of reading, most of her students clamor for the opportunity."

"Imagine if all teachers had her passion, what the level of interest in learning would be," added Lucy.

"You're right, Lucy, it would be fantastic!" said Kip. "Let me tell you about the second type, Connectors.

"Connectors know more people both inside and outside the organization and spend more time in social interaction than the average person. Connectors have an unusual talent for making acquaintances. They spread ideas through the sheer number of people with whom they come in contact. I'm not describing gossips here. Gossips love to spread rumors that may be unsubstantiated and perhaps even hurtful. Rather, Connectors are people who have a special gift for bringing people together.

"And it's not just the number of people Connectors know; it's the broad range of people they count as acquaintances. What makes connectors special is their ability to bridge several social cultures and subcultures; they're comfortable in any number of different worlds."

"Kip, I know who you're describing," remarked Yolanda. "Collectors collect information, while Connectors collect people. They know a lot of people, and, more important, they know how to bring these people together."

"Precisely, Yolanda," resumed Kip. "They have an extraordinary talent for creating what sociologists call the weak tie—friendly yet casual social connections.[2]

Connectors know more people both inside and outside the organization and spend more time in social interaction than the average person. Connectors have an unusual talent for making acquaintances.

"The most amazing Connector I ever met was a man named Milt; everybody called him Uncle Miltie. He worked for the Office of Development and University Relations at my alma mater. His main job was to assist in fund raising for the university. When the university choir traveled, for instance, Milt went along to solicit potential donors who might be attending the concerts.

"What made Uncle Miltie special was his unique ability to remember names. He was the kind of guy who, having met you just once, could years later remember not just your name but the names of your parents, your spouse, your children, their spouses, and their children. It seemed he could store vast amounts of personal information about people and then later recall it with little effort."

"Kip, I think I know another great example of a Connector," interjected Lucy. "Recently I read about Paul Revere, the famous American silversmith and patriot. His ability to connect people enabled him to quickly raise the alarm as the British gathered to march on Lexington. This allowed the Americans, to the utter astonishment of the British troops, to organize fierce resistance to their advance.

"One might assume that astonishing news, such as the British massing to attack, would be enough for the word to spread," she continued. "But such was not the case. Others, who carried the identical message to other parts of the countryside outside Boston, failed to rouse the same response. In short, people already knew Revere and knew him to be well connected. Therefore, they believed what he had to say and responded to the alarm."[3]

"Lucy, every organization has people who possess the same rare gifts as Uncle Milt and Paul Revere," said Kip. "And because they have the talent for collecting people and making connections between them, Connectors are very important to the process of spreading a social epidemic of accountability. But Collectors and Connectors may not necessarily be good persuaders.

"It's Persuaders, the third type of people," continued Kip, "who can really help ignite change and who are particularly adept at convincing others to embrace new ideas. They have the gift of gab and are far more empathetic than most people, more able to connect on an emotional level with people. More important, people find it easy to relate to Persuaders and to the ideas they share.

> *Persuaders have the gift of gab and*
> *are far more empathetic than most people,*
> *more able to connect on an emotional level*
> *with people. More important, people find*
> *it easy to relate to Persuaders and*
> *to the ideas they share.*

"Persuaders have the ability to convince even the toughest skeptics. They are undaunted by objections and excuses. Through sheer enthusiasm, energy, and charm, they are able to win over the doubters. They are far more optimistic than the average person, and they see opportunities where others see problems.

"Persuaders are masters of nonverbal language. They not only 'dance' to their own words; they are able to get others to unconsciously join in the dance with them. Their body language is very expressive; they have charisma. We nod along with them and match the pitch, volume, and tempo of their speech. We lean forward and back as they do. We are not aware of the dance, but we dance along nonetheless. In this way, persuaders seduce us into accepting their ideas; they lift our spirits and make us feel good about having been persuaded."[4]

"I think I know a Persuader," observed Yolanda. "I had a friend who could sell ice to Eskimos. R.J. is a life insurance agent and broker. I didn't tell you before, but I was once in the life insurance business. I did quite well but got tired of the late nights. I'd just gotten married, and it wasn't fun leaving notes for each other.

"Anyway, at the time, when I knew R.J., the old 'agency system' of selling life insurance was beginning to die, and even longtime agents were failing. Yet R.J.'s sales increased every year."

"What set him apart? What made R.J. different?" asked Kip.

"Well, it was a lot of things," replied Yolanda. "First, it didn't hurt that R.J. was tall and good-looking. At just over six feet, two inches and with a dark mane of thick, well-groomed hair, R.J. attracted attention in a crowd. And he always had a slightly crooked grin spreading across his face. He was at ease with himself and at ease with people.

"Years ago, when I worked just down the hall from him, I could hear him through the walls, making calls to set up appointments. He always sounded like he was having fun from the moment he began talking. One day I wandered into his office and asked, 'How is it that you know so many people to call?' He laughed and replied, 'I didn't know a single person I called today.'

"'But you made three appointments with just five phone calls,' I said. 'How'd you do it?' R.J. dropped his head slightly, leaned back in his chair, and said, 'I like talking to people.'

"More than that, R.J. loved his job. He arrived before anyone else in the morning and went home well after everyone else had left for the day. Selling wasn't drudgery for him.

"And R.J. was extraordinarily persuasive. He had the ability to cajole and entice even the most unfriendly and resistant of prospects. He never took on the negativity of others; more often than not, even the most stubborn curmudgeon warmed to his infectious zeal."

"Yolanda, that's a great example," said Kip. "As you might guess, nearly every large organization has at least one Persuader like R.J. They are often cast in the role of head cheerleader like the charismatic new-age guru Steve Jobs of Apple, the legendary Lee Iacocca of Chrysler, or Jan Carlzon of Scandinavian Airlines. Persuaders like these are critical to igniting change. Adding a Persuader to the mix of messengers is like adding gasoline to a fire. Pour a little on and—whoosh! The flames explode."

The four of them laughed.

Kip summarized: "Together with Collectors who find the new ideas and Connectors who broadly spread the word, Persuaders add a spark to the message.

"But the presence of Collectors, Connectors, and Persuaders," said Kip, picking up Pete's thread from earlier, "in an organization can't spread the flames of accountability without Visionary Leaders who champion the philosophy. Without the unwavering advocacy of the senior executive, the freedom-based philosophy is unlikely to stick, and the movement will fail.

"Visionary Leaders feel a personal responsibility for creating a freedom-based organization. They are constantly looking for ways to help their people make the philosophy successful. They do everything they can to protect the organization's long-term financial health.

Visionary Leaders feel a personal responsibility for creating a freedom-based organization. They are constantly looking for ways to help their people make the philosophy successful. They do everything they can to protect the organization's long-term financial health.

"Let me tell you about a wonderful example of just such a Visionary Leader I worked with. Her name is Charlene. She had been a senior-level executive with a large regional manufacturing company that had adopted a freedom-based philosophy. In fact, she played a major role in helping bring the philosophy into that organization. Two years later, she accepted the job as CEO of a smaller manufacturing company in another part of the country.

"When her new company hired her, Charlene's first act was to commission a study of the workplace environment using the Values & Attitude Study (VAS).[5] The results of the study showed that the staff was unhappy and disengaged. When her new operation's scores were contrasted against the worldwide scores, it only confirmed to her the fact that her new company was not competitive. Her financial numbers corresponded to the VAS numbers. Productivity was low and absenteeism high."

"What did she do to turn it around?" asked Lucy.

"With the help of her senior executive team," responded Kip, "she began recruiting Collectors, Connectors, Persuaders, and Visionary Leaders from the ranks to help spread the freedom-based philosophy throughout the organization. By working together, her people were able to significantly reduce the level of Values Tension. Values Tension exists when there's a gap between a person's values and how the operation delivers on those values; the difference is why we call it a Tension Index. When Charlene and her executive team began to recognize the significance of lowering the Values Tension, productivity and other critical measures improved. Lucy, values need to be in alignment before any real productivity changes can be sustainable."

"What happened to their profits?" asked Pete.

"Pete, as their Values Tension decreased, revenue and profit improved," said Kip. "In fact, their Values Tension has dropped by nearly 40 percent since their first study was done three years ago, and profits have improved every year. A lot of hard work and focus by many people have made this organization a great place to work," said Kip with pride.

Pete took a long, close look at Kip; the older man was positively beaming. With a sudden flash of insight, Pete realized that this time with Kip was no accident; it was a gift!

Kip concluded his example: "So, by identifying these four groups of key people, we were able to change our thinking, and ultimately we brought everyone on board. It took them a little over three years to accomplish this. And remember, you do this by recruiting one person at a time. Some come right away to this idea; others hold out because of fear of the unknown. But eventually, if you're patient, you'll be successful."

"There you are!" bellowed Hank Striker in a loud voice. Everyone in the dining car looked up as Hank approached the table. "Hope you don't mind me joining you," he announced to the foursome, "but I promised my friend Yolanda that I'd have breakfast with her." Everyone was startled by the interruption. Yolanda smiled a controlled smile, and the rest were speechless.

"Well, Yolanda, aren't you going to introduce me to your friends?" asked Hank loudly.

As incredible as it seemed, Hank Striker was sucking on an unlit cigar, and it was not yet 10:30 in the morning, Pete observed.

"Sure," said Yolanda, clearing her throat. "I'd like you to meet Lucy Woo, Stan Kiplinger, and Pete Williams." At that, Hank slid into Yolanda's side of the table, overly crowding Lucy and Yolanda with his extra girth.

"Well, this looks like one happy family," said Hank, with some amusement. The others were both motionless and speechless by this intrusion.

Kip took the initiative to speak: "So what takes you to L.A.?"

"A visit to one of my West Coast distributors. They're stealing me blind!"

Kip smiled and said in an almost inaudible voice, "Tell me about that."

And for the next thirty minutes Yolanda's compartment companion, Hank Striker, regaled the foursome with one grisly tale after another of how he was being victimized by some distributor. Pete and Lucy offered no comments or advice but listened in rapt silence.

15

Owning Your Job Means *No* Excuses— The First Step to Freedom

The midmorning sun on the new-fallen snow created a glare that was nearly blinding. One of the waiters approached the booth where the enlarged group was seated and asked, "May I pull the window shade for you?"

Pete and Yolanda, who were next to the window facing into the bright sunlight, nodded appreciatively. After the shade was pulled, the waiter cleared the breakfast dishes and poured them each another cup of coffee.

Kip turned to the waiter and said, "Mr. Striker just joined us. I think he wants breakfast."

Pete took a sip of his coffee and said to Kip, "I really like your description of freedom-based leaders, both the Wise Counsel and the Visionary Leader. But what about staff members—how do you get them to be accountable?"

Striker normally would have waded into the conversation, but he had enough sense to keep quiet and listen.

"I also am interested in this issue," said Lucy, hoping to keep Hank outnumbered at the table. Yolanda sat back, letting Lucy and Pete run block for her.

Kip obliged. Turning politely to Hank Striker he said, "Yesterday, we all met and began talking about a new approach to managing people. I call it a freedom-based philosophy."

Hank couldn't resist responding any longer. "This isn't some hippie notion or something, is it?"

Glaring straight at Hank, Lucy coldly commented, "Mr. Striker, we're pleased that you joined us, but if you would please allow Kip to continue. And no, this has nothing to do with hippies!"

Hank could tell that 'little Lucy Woo' might skewer him on a hibachi if he wasn't careful. "OK, I'll be glad to listen," he said, looking at Lucy with caution in his eyes. Pete just smiled and crossed his arms.

Kip continued as though nothing had happened. "Getting staff members to be accountable starts by giving them the individual freedom to own their jobs. A freedom-based organization encourages individuals to determine the responsibilities they should own by asking four questions."

At that, Kip grabbed a napkin and jotted down the four questions:

1. What responsibilities should I own as part of my existing job?

2. What responsibilities should I not own or give away, because I either do not enjoy doing them or believe I'm not the right person to own this activity?

3. What responsibilities should I share with others, such as team activities?

4. What new responsibilities or activities should I take on that I have never been allowed to do or participate in?

Kip looked up at the others and said, "Answering just these four simple questions gives us the best way for new people and veterans alike to really start becoming accountable. But I have one cautionary note. You'll need to spend some up-front time with your people going through this process of designing their job so that they understand why they're structuring their responsibilities in this way.

"Getting people to own their jobs is critical in creating a freedom-based organization. When people own their jobs, leadership is freed from the need to monitor performance, and the staff is freed from the bonds of being monitored. Instead, leaders expect staff members to own their job responsibilities and to be accountable for their results. And staff members expect leadership to be available when asked for mentoring and for needed resources, but not to own the responsibility for the job."

To Hank, this talk was like being on Mars. Heck, he paid his people's salaries so they took orders from him. What was complicated about that? But he decided to keep his opinions to himself for the time being and to listen.

Pete asked, "Kip, can you give me an example of how owning your job actually works?"

Yolanda said, "I'd be interested in that answer, too."

"Sure," said Kip. "In the mid-1990s, I worked with a midwestern American company in the computer business. Their marketing team was, for the first time, preparing to attend an industry conference outside the United States. Attending this conference in Germany was an important first step toward opening new overseas markets for them.

"As the day of the conference drew near and despite careful scheduling and planning, one of the team members noticed that the tools needed to set up their product display had not been shipped with the rest of the materials."

"That must have sent them into a panic!" cut in Lucy.

"They were, of course, alarmed," continued Kip. "But as soon as Dick, the marketing team leader, became aware of the situation, he called Kim, the shipping department leader, into his office and instructed her to ship the tools via a particular well-known major carrier before the end of the day.

"Kim, who had accumulated years of experience shipping product for the company, said to Dick, 'The carrier you are suggesting is very good. But we have a long-term relationship with another carrier that I've found to be highly reliable and that can guarantee delivery within our time frame at a significantly lower rate.'"

Pete inquired, "How did Dick respond to that?"

"Dick was unmoved," said Kip. "He said, 'I don't care about the cost; these tools have to get there on time. The carrier I want has a reliable tracking system that will allow us to check on delivery before we get to Germany. Ship it with them!'"

"How did Kim feel about being ordered to use Dick's choice of carrier?" asked Yolanda.

"Kim was wounded but stood her ground," Kip replied. "She took a deep breath and in a controlled tone said to Dick, 'I've been analyzing the rates and reliability of different carriers for both foreign and domestic shipments. I track the promptness of their pickup service and how often delivery is made on time. You can believe me when I say that our carrier will get the package there on time and for a lot less money.'

"Dick paused and thought. His neck was on the line if the tools didn't arrive in time for the show."

Hank couldn't resist the impact he thought his comment was going to have on the others: "If I had been Dick and she messed me over, I'd have eaten her for lunch."

"Yes," said Kip calmly, "that's one way of reacting, but luckily Dick chose another route. He knew Kim to be reliable, and he trusted her judgment. Finally, he said, 'Kim, you're the expert on shipping here. I'll leave it to you to choose the carrier.'"

"I'll bet it took a lot of guts for Dick to say that to her," commented Pete, "trusting her like that."

"It did take guts and some humility, too," responded Kip, looking directly at Hank. "Although his initial reaction had been to take command of the situation, Dick remembered that Kim owned the job of shipping at the company, not him. As it turned out, his trust was well placed. The shipment arrived exactly on time, and the company did save a lot of money. In fact, it saved several thousand dollars."

Hank asked, "But what if the tools hadn't gotten to their destination on time? Wasn't your friend Dick taking an awfully big risk in trusting Kim to get the job done?"

"Failure is always a risk, Hank, but you can't expect staff members to be accountable unless you give them responsibility," said Kip.

"You're right," said Lucy, glaring at Hank. "I've been guilty of taking responsibility away from my staff far too often. And, predictably, they haven't been accountable when I've done it."

Lucy pointedly looked at Hank. "I couldn't help overhearing a phone conversation you were having yesterday. It doesn't sound like you trust your people."

Hank took the bait. "That's right, little lady. I pay them—I don't have to trust them. No one messes with me. I'm the boss, and if they don't like it, I'll replace them." Hank's tone rose with every sentence he uttered.

Pete was beginning to get annoyed. "Mr. Striker, I'm offended by your tone to Ms. Woo. And, frankly, your attitude leaves something to be desired. You invited yourself to our table. The least you can do is act civilly. If you can't, then I'd invite you to take it somewhere else." Pete Williams had spent seven years in the United States Marines and was contemplating hitting this man, something he hadn't done in twenty-five years.

"Pete, it's OK. Mr. Striker has a funny way of making friends," intercepted Yolanda.

Hank realized that Pete meant business, and so he smiled nervously and sat back in his seat. "I apologize if I've offended anyone, including you, Ms. Woo. I just get a little frustrated about all this soft, coaching stuff. Hey, I built my company with my bare hands."

Pete continued to look at Hank in an ominous way. "Mr. Striker, I'm sure you work hard. We all do," Pete looked around the table, "but treating people with contempt is foolish and shortsighted. And frankly, no one builds a business alone—including you. I'd be amazed if your people agreed with you. I think they'd believe that they helped."

"OK, you have a point. Sure, they helped, but my name is on the bank line, and I'm on the hook for everything," said Hank.

"Yes, and wouldn't it be nice if you could get the kind of help that you need. Maybe this discussion we're having would be helpful to you," said Pete, in a more conciliatory tone.

Kip guided the discussion back onto the subject, saying, "I often made the same mistake before I figured out what

I was doing to my people by acting in a similar fashion, Mr. Striker. Pete, do you remember when I referred to the international study tool I use called the Values & Attitude Study (VAS)?

"Well, you might be interested in knowing that the data show that about 85 percent of people in nearly every organization claim they come to work each morning intending to be accountable for their choices. Hank, simply stated, 85 percent or more of your employees want to make you proud of them. They want to succeed. But their coworkers report only about half of that number actually behave that way!"[1]

"So you're saying 15 percent of the average staff is so discouraged that they have given up before they even get to work?" asked Lucy. "And another 40 percent or so give up at some point during the workday?"

"Yes, Lucy, those are the numbers," relayed Kip. "The question isn't whether we've hired the right people, because in most cases we have. The question is how to keep people engaged. Keeping them engaged requires us to close the gap between their intent and their actual behavior. Leaders must stop taking responsibility away from people, and staff members must learn to take responsibility, both for their own jobs and for the systems within which they work."

"Could you identify the people who are not working?" asked Hank, in an excited tone.

"Why, so you can fire them?" asked Yolanda.

"Yeah, so I can fire them!" said Hank, grinning.

"That's it!" said Pete. "I'm going to strangle this guy!" Everyone laughed.

"I'm kidding! I'm kidding!" Hank said, laughing. Pete half-smiled, and the group began to relax and listen to Kip.

Kip cleared his throat and began again. "Remember, a Wise Counsel no longer manages or monitors people. In a freedom-based operation, being accountable is not optional; it's part of being a responsible staff member. Put bluntly, those few who are unable or unwilling to take responsibility for their jobs and processes can no longer remain a part of the organization."

"See, I told you people were going to get fired!" said Hank, in a mocking tone.

"Give it a rest, Hank," said Lucy.

"But getting people to be accountable is not accomplished by decree," continued Kip. "Instead, staff members learn to be accountable by gradually taking on new responsibilities while letting go of others. Making this transition requires months, if not years."

"Why so long?" asked Yolanda.

"Well, Yolanda," began Kip, "first people have to understand the choices available to them and the reasons limitations exist; plus they need feedback on the appropriateness of their choices. Those who tend to take on too much need to learn to make more realistic choices. Those who want to take on too little need encouragement and mentoring. Staff members need perspective. And don't forget, it takes time to build competence in new responsibilities. Deciding which responsibilities belong to whom is a cooperative endeavor.

"Deciding which responsibilities individual staff members should not own does not imply that avoiding responsibility is an option. Obviously, this is not the case. But, deciding which responsibilities you should not own gives you the opportunity to discard responsibilities for which you have little enthusiasm, talent, or interest."

Pete interjected, with a smile, "I can think of a few responsibilities I would gladly give up, if given the opportunity."

"Nearly everyone can, Pete," confirmed Kip. "You might conclude that you should not own responsibilities for which you are underqualified; or you might give up responsibilities for which you are overqualified. Besides, hanging onto responsibilities that really should belong to someone else robs another person of the opportunity to develop new competencies and to take on new challenges."

"I agree," said Yolanda, "but don't you think some people hold on to responsibilities to please others or to feed their own egos?" She was looking straight at Hank when she said this.

"What—what?" said Hank, looking at Yolanda good-naturedly. Lucy laughed.

"I think you're right, Yolanda," agreed Kip. "But holding onto responsibilities you shouldn't own creates an unhealthy codependency. Let me give you an example of this very destructive behavior.

"Angel was a classic people pleaser. People loved Angel because she was always helping them. More than helping, she frequently did their work for them. At first, her coworkers were reluctant to accept her offers of help. But, as time went on, virtually everyone came to depend on Angel's help.

"Angel never said no; she frequently stayed late to help enter data and complete reports while everyone else went home. Predictably, Angel eventually became overwhelmed. But, because she often left her own work uncompleted to help others, her supervisor gave her poor marks on her annual review. Soon after that, Angel began missing work frequently. Two months later, she quit."

"How sad to have lost a good person like Angel," said Yolanda. "We have people like Angel in our organization, too. I guess if they had talked about which responsibilities she should own, Angel might still be working at that company."

"Yolanda, I think you're probably right," agreed Lucy. "But in most organizations, the reward for working hard is more work, while the punishment for not working hard is less work. It feels good to be recognized for working hard, and being given more responsibility builds self-esteem. But having people around you who are not pulling their weight is discouraging!"

"Yes, Lucy," said Kip, "so in a freedom-based organization, taking on responsibility to gain power or to please others is not encouraged. Choosing the responsibilities you should and should not own is based on common sense—what's good for the individual, and what's good for the organization. The customer's interests also have to be taken into account."

Once again, Pete took the discussion off in a new direction by saying, "Kip, I'm glad you mentioned the customer in deciding who should or should not own responsibilities. But how is it possible to get people to be accountable to the customer when responsibilities are shared?"

"That's an excellent question, Pete," acknowledged Kip. "Sharing responsibilities is vital to the health of an organization. The key is to get staff members to share responsibility for designing the policies and processes within which they work. When people own those policies and processes, they naturally accept responsibility for how well they work, because *they're* in control.

"And sharing these responsibilities enables staff members to correct problems early on and to avoid failures. In the end, sharing these responsibilities recognizes that every staff member has a part in the success and failure of the organization."

Pete challenged Kip with a question: "You're putting a great deal of trust in the competency and the good intent of people within the organization, aren't you?"

"Yes, I am," conceded Kip, "but getting people to be accountable to each other is possible only when people are able to trust each other completely."

Kip turned to Pete. "I think you said something last night about having served in the marines," said Kip, "so let me give you an example from the Marine Corps of the United States. This particular branch of the United States armed forces more than any other branch prides itself on understanding the importance of complete trust and the relationship and distinction between a single strong leader and shared leadership where trust is the fiber that keeps the group together. 'Semper fidelis,' always faithful, is more than a motto in the Marine Corps; it's a code of survival." Pete nodded in support of what Kip was saying.

Continuing, Kip said, "Pete, as you know, the Marine Corps makes a clear distinction between teams who actually share responsibility in an equal capacity and work groups where responsibility remains with a single leader. In an article titled 'Firing Up the Front Line,' Jon Katzenbach and Jason Santamaria elaborate." Kip began to read an article he had pulled from his briefcase that was under the table.

One of the most common—and damaging—occurrences in business are executives putting together single-leader work groups and calling them teams. Usually

197

the practice is unintentional; most executives don't know the difference between the two arrangements. . . .

Real teams are rare. Most work in business is done by single leader work groups, which rely entirely on leaders for purpose, goals, motivation, and assignments; each member is accountable solely to the leader. . . .

A real team, by contrast, draws its motivation more from its mission and goals than from its leader. Members work together as peers and hold one another accountable for the group's performance and results. In a real team, no individual member can win or lose; only the group can succeed or fail. . . .

The Marines are masters at distinguishing between single leader work groups and teams, partly because the Corps maintains a culture of extreme clarity—you can't be vague about battle directives.[2]

Kip lifted his eyes from the article and looked at the group as a whole. "While survival in an organization may not be a matter of life and death as it is in the Marine Corps," explained Kip, "learning to share responsibility and to trust one another completely is just as important. Conversely, sharing responsibility in a single-leader work group is impossible because, as the marines have learned, the single leader alone bears ultimate responsibility for the work group's results.

"Kip, I can see your point if your people are in actual combat, but do you really think sharing responsibility is possible in the business world?" asked Lucy.

"Yes, I do, Lucy," affirmed Kip. "Let me give you another example. In the business of major league baseball, when a team fails to produce enough wins to suit the owners, the manager pays the price with his job. It doesn't matter that the team may have been decimated by injuries or that the players are not as skilled as those on other teams; in major league baseball managers are responsible for winning games.

"Likewise, in corporate America, CEOs who fail to produce enough wins eventually lose their jobs. Economic downturns, industry slumps, and the loss of key people are irrelevant to owners and stockholders who expect bottom-line results from the CEO."

"What's wrong with shareholders expecting a CEO to get an organization to perform? Isn't that his or her job?" disputed Hank.

"Of course it is," agreed Kip. "But freedom-based organizations understand that improving organizational results depends on getting people to work well together. That's why getting people to understand the organization's vision and to set appropriate goals is so important! The CEO's real job is creating the conditions for his or her team to perform well under any conditions.

"Changing CEOs or staff might do nothing to address these conditions. Learning to work together and to share responsibilities, on the other hand, does. Let me give you an example."

"I don't know," said Hank interrupting. "That seems like a real stretch to me. Why shouldn't the CEO be on the hook?" He sat back to hear the answer to his question.

"You'd be right, Hank, if the CEO was the ultimate decision maker and controller of everything that goes on," said Kip.

"Kip's got a point," said Pete, in Kip's defense. "I'm a CEO, and I must tell you, I may be responsible for the bottom line, but I sure can't affect everything that affects the bottom line as we're presently organized. So this freedom-based approach makes a lot of sense. Why? Because I see this system attaching a lot more people to the bottom line."

"And that's the key," pointed out Kip. "In a freedom-based workplace, our efforts are centered around including everyone in the bottom line. In a control-based environment, we isolate people."

"Exactly, and it's that isolation that undermines the bottom line," said Lucy with satisfaction. "I now see a major distinction between the two approaches."

"Kip, could you give me an example of a freedom-based approach that connects staff members to the bottom line and makes them accountable?" asked Yolanda.

"My pleasure," said Kip. "Joe, a twenty-eight-year-old employee with a food-processing company, decided that he'd wanted to learn to do budgeting for the part of the production line on which he had worked for ten years. He had barely finished high school, but with the encouragement of his coworkers and a Wise Counsel named Joyce, he learned fundamental business skills such as reading a profit-and-loss statement and preparing budgets."

"Amazing," said Hank, shaking his head. "Give me Joe's last name—I want him to work for me. He sounds like a young me!"

"Sorry, I can't do that," smiled Kip. "After he'd mastered these skills, Joe took on the responsibility of teaching the rest of the team how to prepare the production line budget. Together with help from Joyce, who had previously been responsible for preparing the budget, the team developed a creative solution to a recurring budget problem that had plagued the production line for years. And, for the first time in their company history, a group of frontline production workers shared responsibility for preparing and monitoring their own budget!" Kip sat back and saw the disbelief on Hank's face.

Then Hank bellowed, "Now *that's* accountability!"

For the first time in Hank Striker's business life, he was hearing an alternative to his way of doing things. No, this wasn't "hippie talk." Maybe this older man knew something after all, something Hank Striker could learn.

16

Designing Your Job Means
You Have the Power to Choose!

The waiter approached the table to clear the last of the breakfast dishes. "Folks, we'll be serving lunch in about an hour," he said. "Would you like a menu?"

Kip answered, "What do you all think?"

"This is as good a place as any to spend a few more hours talking," said Lucy. "Frankly, I'd rather sit here than go back to the compartment." Yolanda agreed, and Pete chimed in, "Fine with me."

"Well, I don't have anything more important to do, so why not?" said Hank.

Pete asked, "Kip, I was thinking about helping my people take responsibility for their jobs. And I think I understand how to do that, but I'm still not clear about how to get them to take responsibility for the organization's systems. Could you tell me how you do that?"

"Now that's something I'm interested in, too," said Lucy.

"Pete," began Kip, "it's all about giving people the personal responsibility to own the systems. We do that by creating flexible systems that give individuals a great degree of freedom to serve their customers.

"Designing flexibility into your systems begins by asking two questions." Kip held up two fingers. "First, we need to ask, 'Who's our customer?' and second, 'Do the existing systems support or restrict our ability to serve our customer?' Now, this is no longer management's job, it's everyone's job to answer at every level of the operation.

Designing Flexible Systems

- Who's our customer?

- Do the existing systems support or restrict our ability to serve our customer?

"As I said earlier, a freedom-based organization designs every system to provide maximum flexibility in order to better serve customers. Sometimes this means building in redundancy, not removing it. Conversely, control-based management systems are designed primarily for maximum efficiency, and often they put into place systems that maximize resources but poorly serve the customer."

"I know all about that," said Yolanda, shaking her head in dismay. "All you have to do is call up any government agency. Do you get a live voice on the other end? Not on your life. You get an answering machine."

Pete interjected in commiseration. "When's the last time you called a bank to get your balance? You get the same thing—an answering machine. It's incredible the number of buttons you have to push. And when you finally get to talk to a real, live person, they ask you for your account number all over again!" Everyone laughed in unison.

"Yeah, and what I want to know is, who's the genius who started all this?" said Hank.

"Why, so you can fire the guy?" said Lucy, laughing.

"Maybe," said Hank with a wink.

"Yes," said Kip. "Often when we design for maximum efficiency—with the bank and the government phone systems being great examples—we restrict our ability to serve customers. And we underserve them, not intentionally, but the net effect is the same. By requiring our staff to follow any system, policy, or procedure blindly—whether doing so serves customers or not—we undermine our organization's reputation.

"Lucy, I'm not talking about getting rid of sensible processes or approaches that work, but leave that decision up to the frontline people. I'm talking about blindly following procedures that make no sense or that don't support your people's goals and the Keen Internal Vision."

"You know, you're right, Kip," said Pete. "Customers judge our organization based on a single interaction with just one employee. To that customer, that employee *is* the company. If the interaction is positive, the customer concludes that our company is a good one. If the interaction is negative. . . ." Pete raised his palms upward and dropped his head to one side to emphasize his point to the group.

"I agree with you, Pete," said Yolanda. "Put bluntly, customers don't really care why an organization's systems exist or how they're supposed to work. They just want good products and good customer service—when they want it!"

"Yeah, and without excuses," said Hank, poking his finger toward Kip.

"So providing customers with high-quality products and services," said Kip, "is greatly enhanced by designing flexible systems with the full participation of the staff who live within the systems. After all, who knows your customers better than the people on the front lines who serve them?" said Kip.

Pete added, "That's a good point, Kip. As CEO, I rarely interact with customers anymore unless they are really upset."

"That's a common situation for senior executives," concurred Kip. "And it's a compelling argument for why it's so important for CEOs to continually encourage staff members to modify the systems that don't meet their customers' needs. But changes shouldn't be made willy-nilly. Rather, the senior executive needs to remind folks that just because the systems work well for most customers doesn't mean they work well for all customers."

Lucy nodded, "We've been trying to design the perfect customer service process for years, without success. Now I see how my organization can add value to that design with our existing clients and with new ones when they come along."

Kip nodded at Lucy and continued. "A luminary on the subject of customer service is Hal Rosenbluth, CEO of

Rosenbluth Travel, a billion-dollar travel business. Hal talks about treating employees like customers. His approach is simple: Treat your employees well, and they in turn will treat your customers well. Conversely, treat your employees poorly, and they will treat your customers poorly."

At this, Hank noticeably perked up. Now Kip had his undivided attention. "Here's how Rosenbluth puts it," Kip said. Grabbing a piece of paper from his briefcase, he began to read aloud:

> When news spread of our company's 7,500-percent growth in revenue over the past fifteen years (from $20 million to $1.5 billion while maintaining profitability above industry standards), we began to be literally inundated with requests to share our "secret" of success. Our secret is controversial. It centers on our basic belief that companies must put their people—not their customers—first. You might wonder how our clients feel about this. For our people, the clients are priority number one. Our company has built a solid reputation in the field of customer service (in fact, our client retention rate is 96 percent), but we have actually done it by focusing inside, on our own people.[1]

"To become a world-class customer service organization," Kip continued, "Rosenbluth counsels, 'organizations must first turn their attention to serving internal customers.'[2] And serving internal customers requires systems that make it easy to serve external customers. This requires flexibility."

"Kip, by advocating flexibility, you're not promoting permissiveness, are you?" asked Lucy.

"No, I'm not," responded Kip looking at Hank, "nor am I suggesting that the systems should be soft, fuzzy, or ill defined. Rather, I'm arguing that flexible structures are designed, monitored, and modified by the staff members who work within them to meet the needs of customers.

"One of the key indicators of the potential success of this approach occurs when the lion's share of the folks who are involved and touched by the change welcome it. Ultimately, you need to look at all policies and systems as works in progress, not sacred cows. And the less involvement you as a leader have in the development of any new approach, the better. People will more readily embrace changes if they are the ones who introduce it to you!"

Ultimately, you need to look at all policies and systems as works in progress, not sacred cows.

"Well, that's a lot different than the way we make changes to our systems now," said Pete, "but I can see how important it would be in a freedom-based operation."

Hank Striker was taking all this talk in. He remained silent. No more wisecracks, no more stupid remarks.

"Speaking of changes to the system," interjected Pete, "I'm guessing that the most politically volatile change in a freedom-based operation is to the compensation system. Certainly, there ought to be a relationship between compensation and the market value of each job."

"Sure," said Kip, "in a freedom-based organization, compensation systems are designed primarily to encourage staff members to take on greater responsibilities. And people are rewarded for their ability to transfer knowledge and experience to other staff members.

In a freedom-based organization, compensation systems are designed primarily to encourage staff members to take on greater responsibilities. And people are rewarded for their ability to transfer knowledge and experience to other staff members.

"At Johnsonville Foods, for instance, compensation is spread over four pay ranges, depending on one's range of influence."

"That's a different way of paying people," noted Yolanda.

"You bet, Yolanda," continued Kip. "It suggests a different way to create an incentive approach for people that is positive and constructive and doesn't include bribing them."

Hank interrupted. "Hey, I know Johnsonville. They've got great brats and sausage!"

"I will sure agree with that," exclaimed Kip. Turning and grabbing a clean piece of paper, he took out his pen and began writing. "Level 1 pays people who are able to manage themselves in their own jobs. If you can't do this within the first ninety days, you can't stay at Johnsonville Foods!

"At level 2, pay increases as staff members are able to influence other members of their work group.

"Level 3 pays staff members more for being able to influence others throughout the entire organization. And, at level 4, members are rewarded for being able to influence the entire industry."

Pete thought for a moment and then asked, "You're saying that at Johnsonville, pay is not necessarily tied to job titles and promotions."

"That's exactly what I'm saying, Pete," said Kip pointedly. "But I'm not saying Johnsonville's approach is the only way to pay people. No one compensation program or approach is appropriate everywhere."

Yolanda nodded her head in agreement with Kip's last statement. "That's for sure."

"Here's another example of what I think you're talking about, Kip," said Lucy. "At Egon Zehnder International, an executive search firm, seniority and company-wide results determine the pay. Their approach is a little out of the ordinary, I know. That's why it caught my interest, because it *was* so different from the current thinking in the compensation."

Pete turned to Lucy. "Great, tell us about it."

"Egon Zehnder, the founder and retired chairman," began Lucy excitedly, "explains his unique approach to paying people this way. Let me see if I can remember how he said it. Oh, yeah: 'Today, most consulting firms, law firms, and so forth, consider seniority irrelevant—and occasionally something much worse. They believe pay should be based on performance and, more specifically, individual performance.'

"'At Egon Zehnder International (EZI), we prefer to stick with the old-fashioned way to pay. In addition to base salaries, the firm gives partners equal shares of the profit and another set of profit shares that are adjusted only for length of tenure as partner.'[3]

"Listen to these results," continued Lucy. "Using this old-fashioned system, EZI has an annual turnover rate of just 2 percent, while the industry average is 30 percent! This difference in turnover costs EZI's competition a bundle of money, while bringing significant dollars to their bottom line. EZI reports billings and profits that have expanded steadily for thirty-seven years."[4]

"But why does EZI's old-fashioned compensation system work so well?" asked Yolanda.

"Zehnder says there are two main reasons," Lucy answered. "First, the system attracts people who are inclined to collaborate with others and encourages the sharing of information. Second, the system requires the firm to look for people who desire long-term employment. As a result, EZI retains very experienced consultants who, because of their numerous contacts, are able to match executives to organizations exceptionally well."

Kip summed up what his and Lucy's examples implied: "It would seem then that regardless of how you design your compensation system, great care should be taken to pay people fairly based on how much they contribute to the success of the organization. To that end, freedom-based organizations try to design compensation systems that do not create extrinsic distractions."

Freedom-based organizations try to design compensation systems that do not create extrinsic distractions.

Yolanda pondered Kip's comment for a moment before responding. "So, regardless of how you design your compensation system, freedom-based organizations pay people based on what they contribute. I can see the logic of that approach, but how do you let people know how much they're contributing?"

"Let me take a crack at that," begged Lucy. "I think the worst way to let people know how they're doing is by using a performance appraisal."

Kip interrupted Lucy, saying, "Excuse me for cutting in, Lucy, but I keep this quotation around for just such occasions." He pulled a tattered file from his briefcase where he kept his oft-used quotes. Pete glanced at Hank assuming that whatever this quote was, it would set Hank off.

Kip began reading:

[Performance appraisals impede] the reception of feedback, and there is no solid evidence that they motivate people or lead to meaningful improvement. Due to its inherent flaws, appraisal produces distorted and unreliable data about the contribution of employees. Consequently, the resulting documentation is not useful for staffing decisions and often does not hold up in court. Too often, appraisal destroys human spirit and, in the span of a thirty-minute meeting, can transform a vibrant, highly committed employee into a demoralized, indifferent wallflower who reads the want ads on the weekend.[5]

"Put bluntly, performance appraisals don't work!" said Pete.

"Yes, Pete, they don't work and should be abandoned," agreed Kip.

"I love performance appraisals!" said Hank, with a look of astonishment.

Pete continued down the same path: "To quote Chuck Colson of the Nixon administration, 'When you've got a hold of their you-know-whats, their hearts and minds *will* follow!'"

"Yeah," Lucy responded, "he and the rest of that paranoid gang ended up in federal prison."

There was dead silence for a moment, then Yolanda wondered aloud, "Why don't performance appraisals work, and what do you replace them with?"

Hank had not responded to any of their comments, which surprised Pete greatly.

"Yolanda, they don't work because most performance appraisal systems are a form of judgment and control. Basically, they're an attempt to manipulate behavior," said Lucy.

"Right, Lucy!" said Kip, smiling, in recognition of his ally. "On the other hand, Yolanda, freedom-based organizations think of staff members as partners. By shifting the focus from performance appraisal to personal development, staff members take ownership for both their past performance and their future skill development. This kind of feedback is given daily. Periodic appraisals are eliminated. Freedom-based organizations think of staff members as partners. By shifting the focus from performance appraisals to personal development plans that the individual creates, staff members take ownership for both their past performance and their future skill development.

> *By shifting the focus from performance appraisals to personal development plans that the individual creates, staff members take ownership for both their past performance and their future skill development.*

"Periodic performance appraisals put people on the defensive and create a passive-aggressive relationship between boss and employee."

Pete added fuel to the discussion. "I recently read an article by Max DePree, chairman and CEO of Herman Miller Inc., a furniture maker recognized by *Fortune* magazine as one of the best companies in America to work for. He suggests that an effective approach might involve an annual planning session asking questions like these:

- "Please prepare a brief review, one or two pages, of how you feel you have done in comparison to your annual plan. What is the most important achievement in your area?

- "Describe your personal plans for continuing education and development for the coming year.

- "Please think about ways for us to approach our accountability (with many others) for the future of the corporation and our joint accountability for your future career in the corporation. What kind of changes will be required by the growth picture we are plotting?

- "Please identify five key projects and/or goals you have as a key leader at Herman Miller and in which you feel I can be of help or support."[6]

Kip recognized that Pete and the others were now fast becoming total converts to the freedom-based philosophy—well, all except perhaps Hank.

Kip pointed out, "Treating staff members as partners includes providing opportunities for long-term career development as well. Of course, not all organizations can provide the opportunity for every staff member to advance his or her career within the organization over an entire working lifetime."

Turning to Yolanda, Kip continued, "And, of direct interest to you, Yolanda, this is the direction I'd say the incentive industry could entertain for their future value-added offerings."

Lucy piped up, saying, "The consulting industry, like many others, is notorious for turnover. My experience suggests that very few of our people can expect to be with us for their entire careers."

Pete commented on Lucy's point. "That's the case in most organizations. But I think what Kip is saying to us is, helping staff members develop the skills they need for their next position, whether it's within our organization or elsewhere, provides benefits to both the employee and the employer."

"Precisely," said Kip. "When staff members benefit from a growing sense of confidence and a greater depth of knowledge, the organization benefits by not trapping them in jobs they've outgrown or that have outgrown them."

"You're not suggesting we spend our time helping our people develop skills that might take them out of our organization, are you?" questioned Lucy in astonishment.

"That's exactly what I'm suggesting," Kip replied. "Demonstrating an unselfish interest in helping staff members develop long-term career skills is an excellent way to gain their loyalty. This approach creates a bilateral agreement in which the organization accepts the responsibility for providing long-term career growth opportunities, while, at the same time, the individual accepts the responsibility for their own career development."

"Are you all from Mars?" asked Hank incredulously, unable to contain himself any longer.

Pete looked at Hank again with his Marine Corps stare and said, "Maybe we are, but this makes a lot of sense."

"And maybe, just maybe, I'll have someone beam *you* up, Hank!" said Lucy, with a wry smile.

Kip wanted the group to get back on point. "Pete, here's an example from the beverage industry. The typical career of a soft drink or beer delivery driver ends when their back gives out, usually some time in their forties. Planning for the driver's next nondriver position begins the day they're hired. This might involve planning a transition to some other position within the company, such as sales and marketing, management, or support. The transition might just as easily be to a whole new career outside the company.

"Regardless of the career track chosen, the newly hired delivery driver understands that driving a delivery truck is not a job that will last forever. They take ownership of preparing for an inevitable change in jobs, just like a professional athlete would. The point is that developing people is good for them and good for the business."

"So by helping people develop their skills, individuals become responsible for their own futures," added Pete.

"I've got another question for you, Kip," chimed in Lucy. "What about the organization's internal communications systems? How do you get people to take ownership of them?"

"In an increasingly technological society," said Kip, "we've come to rely more and more on electronic means of communication to solve that problem. But using electronic communications systems in the wrong way can be detrimental. I recently picked up an article on just this subject. In it, Edward M. Hallowell, instructor of psychiatry at Harvard Medical School, points out that e-mail and voice-mail are poor substitutes for face-to-face conversations."[7]

"I absolutely agree," interjected Yolanda wholeheartedly. "In fact a friend of mine who worked at Microsoft in the early years said that e-mail at Microsoft was viewed as a contact sport." Everyone laughed, including Hank.

"Now that paints a picture, doesn't it?" said Kip, smiling.

"Yeah, but I've found that many of my people will do almost anything not to deal directly with people!" observed Pete.

"That's true, Pete, but Hallowell tells us *why* that's true. 'Human moments' require energy, energy that we sometimes lack due to our harried, overextended existence. Even when face-to-face exchanges are brief and businesslike, they require our complete attention. We must put aside anything else we're doing to engage effectively with another human being.

Lucy countered, "But you've got to admit that electronic forms of communication have significantly increased the speed of information transmission and the volume of information available to us."

Kip acquiesced, "I'll give you that, Lucy. But while adding convenience, they've also deluged us with daily communications.

"Freedom-based organizations are careful to keep human moments in mind when designing their communications systems. Pete, it's essential that standards of conduct for meetings, e-mail, voice-mail, telephone conversations, memos, and other forms of communication be established. The challenge is to think of how others will perceive the information they're receiving and to design the systems with human moments in mind."

"Enough about the people stuff; how about quality?" added Lucy.

"Lucy, nearly every American organization has implemented some kind of quality initiative," said Kip. Lucy nodded in agreement.

"Quality initiatives of every type," continued Kip, "have played an important role in our evolving economy as organizations have tried to become more efficient and more competitive. Yet what the quality initiatives have often left out is the human element. Even Deming wasn't able to get his message totally across."

"Maybe," proposed Lucy, "that's because quality initiatives are designed by engineers and statisticians whose intentions are good, but who find it difficult to deal with people."

"You could be right, Lucy," Kip assented. "Still, freedom-based organizations gladly embrace quality initiatives provided they don't impose manipulative forms of controls on the people who must work within them. In a freedom-based organization, the people who are accountable for quality design the processes and measure their own work.

"In an article by the retired chairman and CEO of Harley-Davidson, Rich Teerlink, he writes about the importance of creating an organization where 'decisions and accountability are owned by all.' Here's what he says:

> It's important for people to understand that even if you are hardwired, like me, to be a leader who shares power rather than exerts it—even if you set out to be a listener and a team player—the command-and-control model is hard to avoid. That's because the top management job carries certain expectations on behalf of employees, colleagues, and the outside world. It takes trust on the part of employees and discipline on the part of the leader to push back on those traditional expectations and create a company where decisions and accountability are owned by all.[8]

"Teerlink clearly understands the importance of people 'owning' the quality initiatives and measurement systems. He concludes:

Everybody hasn't fully bought into the inclusive approach. We still have some people who think they know all the answers, but these people are getting fewer in number. We still have people who just want to bring their bodies and not their whole selves, mind included, to work. But their ranks are dwindling, too. We've been transforming ourselves since the buyout and will still be at it ten years from now. It is a journey that will never end unless we let it.[9]

"Deming got us to fix the processes," Kip continued, "but other TQM gurus didn't listen to his plea to treat people with dignity, trust, and respect. The other gurus led us to fix the processes, but we ignored the people responsible for making the processes work."

Kip nodded with pride. He was witnessing Pete, Lucy, and Yolanda growing as freedom-based philosophers.

As for Hank Striker, Kip felt like he was hoping for a miracle.

17

Finding Great People

The time was approaching 1:30, and everyone seemed to be aching for a stretch break.

As Pete and Kip walked down the corridor, they noticed Hank sitting in his compartment, talking on his cell phone. Deep in conversation, he was oblivious to Kip and Pete passing by.

"We're still several hours out of L.A.," he shouted into the phone. "I need a car to pick me up at the station and take me to the hotel. And I want our first meeting to start promptly at nine o'clock. And I want everybody to be there, ready to report."

Hank's voice was soon obliterated by the clatter of wheels on the track, as the two men continued down the train car corridor.

"That guy reminds me of my old boss," Pete reminisced. "He was always issuing orders—a real son of a gun, if you know what I mean. I vowed that if I were ever in charge, I wouldn't behave like he did."

"I know what you mean," said Kip, smiling. "I had a boss just like him, too. In fact, early in my career, my management style looked a lot like Hank's. I thought that was how you were supposed to act if you were a manager. But by emulating my boss, some of my best people either didn't stick around very long or openly rebelled. Most of the rest seemed to go along with my orders passively. There were a few good performers I could really count on, but I was constantly frustrated that I couldn't get most of the others to be more accountable."

"Kip," said Pete, "once again, you're very closely describing my current situation. And although I think I know how you're going to answer this question—how did you change your situation?"

"You mean my death spiral?!" said Kip, with some amusement, then he got serious. "Pete, the only subject we still haven't covered in any detail is finding great people for a freedom-based operation."

"I absolutely agree," related Pete. "In fact, when you strip everything else away, the business we're all in is the people business! I often reflect on a quote that I believe is very important: 'Ideas motivate man and . . . it is these ideas which create history. A society without ideas has no history. It merely exists.' Maybe that suggests we are what we think and that without our thoughts we merely exist. I believe that's what author Max Dimont was suggesting by this comment."

"So organizations need people with ideas who aren't afraid to challenge the status quo," formulated Pete.

"Pete, that's a great insight!" marveled Kip. "Every organization that realizes they're in the people business understands they need great people—people who can own their job and own the systems they create.

"A key barometer of a freedom-based organization is whether their people are motivated more by wages and job security or by interesting work. If it's interesting work, you've got it made! Let me see if I can give you an example of what I mean."

Just then Lucy and Yolanda met them in the corridor. "Hi, guys," said Lucy. "Where's the Neanderthal?"

"He's on the phone making life hell for his assistant," said Pete, laughing.

"Well, that's better than him sitting with us," Yolanda said with a smirk.

"Now, now—let's play nice," Kip said, laughing.

"Kip was about to tell me one of his interesting stories," said Pete. "He wanted to give me an example of how important it is to be happy at what you do."

"Great, I could use a good story. Let's get a table," said Lucy.

Kip began: "An award-winning Hollywood screenwriter, who was a very sensitive social activist, was being wooed by a big television producer who had a reputation for producing shows that were insensitive to important social issues. The TV producer had tried everything to get an appointment with the writer but had had no luck. Finally, in desperation the producer conned the screenwriter's assistant into telling him when the writer was making his next plane trip so he could wangle a seat next to the writer on the same flight.

"The producer waited until almost everyone had boarded before he entered the cabin and tried to pretend that his being there was a coincidence. But the writer wasn't buying any of it—he was furious. The flight was full, and the writer couldn't change seats. He knew the producer had him trapped.

"It sounds like something Striker would do," interjected Lucy, with a grin.

"After the producer was seated," Kip continued, "he said, 'Listen, I really want you to write this series. So I'll make you a deal, OK? If you'll just write the pilot, I won't ask you to write any more episodes. If the series is as successful as I know it will be with you writing the pilot, I'll cut you in on the royalties for the entire run of the series, and you'll make so much money you'll never have to write again!'"

"That had to be the worst thing the producer could have said!" Pete laughed.

"Of course it was, Pete. Instead of appealing to the writer's intrinsic love of writing and the challenge of creating a new series that would make a social difference, such as *All in the Family* did back in the seventies for race relations, the producer foolishly tried to appeal to the screenwriter's financial greed!"

"I wish I could find people like that writer," said Pete, "who are more interested in doing work they care about and in making a difference than they are in only making money."

"Pete, as hard as it is to believe," explained Kip, "nearly every human being wants to do work he or she cares about. They want to make a difference. Finding people with the desire and the ability to make a difference is not as difficult as you might imagine. There are people working for you right now who want desperately to make a difference, but many of them, because of the control-based environment in which they work, have lost their interest and enthusiasm."

There are people working for you right now who want desperately to make a difference, but many of them, because of the control-based environment in which they work, have lost their interest and enthusiasm.

"That's the real message regarding incentives, isn't it?" added Yolanda.

Kip nodded.

"Let Kip go on," said Pete.

"There's landmark research," Kip continued, "showing that high-achieving staff members list interesting work as their most important job attribute, not job security or good wages.[1] Yet, we also know that even people who list job security and good wages first were initially looking for interesting work."

There's landmark research showing that high-achieving staff members list interesting work as their most important job attribute, not job security or good wages.

"OK, Kip, I really don't need much convincing at this point," remarked Pete. "How do I find great people who are motivated by interesting work?"

"Since they're already working for you," explained Kip, you simply have to know how to identify them. Here's how: Great people fall into one of three work styles. The first are what I call 'Heroes'; the second, 'Mavericks'; and the third, 'Nine-to-Fivers.'

"One of the best work styles of great people is the Hero. Heroes exhibit extraordinary selflessness, bringing people together and taking great delight in helping others succeed. They are happiest when cooperation is high. Heroes are very comfortable with partnering and are able to keep their egos in check. Heroes allow others to step forward, as they are willing and able, and yet Heroes are perceptive enough to know when to lead. Heroes understand the importance of bringing new people and new ideas into the organization."

> **Heroes:** *Exhibit extraordinary selflessness, bringing people together and taking great delight in helping others succeed. They are happiest when cooperation is high. Heroes are very comfortable with partnering and are able to keep their egos in check.*

"We seem a little short on heroes in my organization right now. What are the other two work styles?" asked Pete.

"The second work style of great people is the Maverick," said Kip. Unlike Heroes, Mavericks prefer to be independent. Most Mavericks tend to gravitate to jobs where the bulk of their time may be spent working alone. They are often more interested in creatively pursuing ideas than in interacting with others. Mavericks tend to push change; they like to champion and explore new ideas.

"They're not content with the status quo, preferring to find new ways of doing things even when the old ways have worked very well. While Heroes are just as capable of being creative, Mavericks need more opportunity for creativity in their jobs.

"I think of myself as a Maverick," said Lucy. Yolanda nodded her head and said, "You go, girl!" The two ladies laughed.

Mavericks: *Prefer to be independent. Most Mavericks tend to gravitate to jobs where the bulk of their time may be spent working alone. They are often more interested in creatively pursuing ideas than in interacting with others. Mavericks tend to push change; they like to champion and explore new ideas.*

"The final work style of great people is the Nine-to-Fiver," continued Kip. "Nine-to-Fivers are the solid citizens who work hard from nine to five and do their very best while at work, but they may be reluctant to take risks. Nine-to-Fivers are the backbone of the labor force."

"I imagine," said Lucy, "that the biggest challenge for a Nine-to-Fiver is taking leadership."

"Yes, they do tend to follow rather than to lead," responded Kip. "Nine-to-Fivers need the encouragement of Heroes and Mavericks to take leadership when it's appropriate."

Nine-to-Fivers: *Are the solid citizens who work hard from nine to five and do their very best while at work, but they may be reluctant to take risks. Nine-to-Fivers are frequently the backbone of the labor force.*

"Our Nine-to-Fivers," said Pete, sounding somewhat discouraged, "will take a good deal of encouraging to become leaders."

"Pete," Kip went on, "there's a fourth work style of great people who have become discouraged. They're called 'Dissidents.' They feel they've been betrayed, and that's when this work style emerges among your Heroes, Mavericks, and Nine-to-Fivers. Nearly everyone, when they get frustrated and angry, feels like a Dissident from time to time."

Dissidents: *Feel they've been betrayed, and that's when this work style emerges among your Heroes, Mavericks, and Nine-to-Fivers. Nearly everyone, when they get frustrated and angry, feels like a Dissident from time to time.*

"Even CEOs get frustrated enough to act like Dissidents sometimes," commented Pete, with some personal self-discovery.

"You bet they do!" agreed Kip. "Chronic Dissidents, the most problematic of the Dissidents, feel frustrated and angry most of the time. They are often actively resistant and may feel justified in withholding truth and trust, and even in touching dishonest dollars. They frequently have formed negative patterns of behavior that are so ingrained that a change in behavior is only a remote possibility. In fact, a Chronic Dissident's behavior may be so damaging to themselves and to others that to allow them to remain risks the health of the organization."

"What about our friend Hank?" asked Yolanda. "What category would you place him in?"

"Your guess is as good as mine," said Kip.

"I'd say that Hank is a Maverick," said Pete.

"I'd tend to agree with you," said Lucy. "Even though he says some awful things, I don't think he's a Dissident, but he could be."

"Yes, any of us could be under the right circumstances," said Kip. "Allow me to continue. In a freedom-based organization, leaders accept that Dissident behavior exists from time to time but that most Dissident behavior is really a symptom of a frustration brought on by the work environment. By addressing these work environment issues openly and honestly, staff members can work out their frustrations in a constructive manner."

"So, Kip, what percentage of people in a typical organization are Heroes, Mavericks, Nine-to-Fivers, and Dissidents?" asked Pete.

"On the average, a little fewer than 40 percent see themselves as Heroes, just over 32 percent see themselves as Mavericks, and about 26 percent view themselves as Nine-to-Fivers. Only about 2 percent identify themselves as Dissidents."[2]

"So, how come I don't see 98 percent great people, if that's true?" asked Lucy.

Kip shook his head slowly. "It's really quite very sad, isn't it? When a staff member's expectations and the realities of the job don't match, he or she tends to become discouraged and will shut down." More upbeat, he added, "But when great people are able to do interesting work, pursue lofty goals, and work with people who share their passion for achievement, something very special occurs."

"And when it doesn't, they bail out," said Pete.

"Yes, Pete," agreed Kip. "I know one lady in Cannon Beach, Oregon, who became a best-selling author after she was turned down for a very well-earned promotion. She was told that because she was a woman, the director level was all she would ever achieve. This was before all the court cases and the changes we witnessed in the eighties and nineties."

"Then, there was a concrete ceiling for talented women," said Lucy.

"Now they call it a glass ceiling," said Yolanda.

"You're right, Yolanda," said Kip, "this tragedy still exists in many organizations. A recent study was commissioned by *Forbes Small Business* magazine to find out why top-performing women executives leave high-paying jobs. While a full two-thirds of those surveyed rated the opportunity to earn more money as their second goal, a staggering 77 percent of top women executives indicated that they opted to strike out on their own for the 'opportunity to take risks.'"[3]

"Guys, speaking as a woman, it is not just about taking risk," commented Yolanda. "I wanted to be treated with fairness and be allowed to succeed or fail regardless of my gender. That was the reason I left my old company."

Kip smiled and nodded. "It's really that simple, isn't it? Set high standards of personal behavior, expect people to be great, and give everyone an opportunity."

Pete sat back and looked for a moment at the passing countryside. "Kip, I want to thank you for all you've shared with us. I've got a lot to think about and a lot to do if I'm going to make the changes necessary to become a freedom-based operation."

"It's been a pleasure, Pete," acknowledged Kip. "If there's anything I can do to help you, all you have to do is ask."

"I, too, want to thank you Kip," said Lucy. "May I have your card? I think we have some more talking to do. Who knows—I may be your business partner some day."

"Me, too, Kip," said Yolanda. "Your ideas are really intriguing, and I would like to continue talking about this."

Kip reached into his pocket, pulled out a few business cards, and handed them around to his companions. He turned to the trio and said, "I guess we all need to get back to our compartments and grab our bags. Have a great holiday season."

E P I L O G U E

PETE WILLIAMS: A NEW JOURNEY BEGINS

Several hours later, the train made its way into the heart of Los Angeles. As it slowed, the steward roused the two men slumped in their seats by tapping gently on the door of compartment 417-C. "Gentlemen, we're about to arrive in Los Angeles. You'll be disembarking in about ten minutes. It was good seeing you again, Mr. Kiplinger. Thank you both for traveling with us!"

Pete sat up in his lounge chair, stretched, and wiped the sleep from his eyes. He reached across to shake Kip's hand. "Kip, I've got to get started on this. I'd sure appreciate it if you could clear some time this week to meet with me, if your schedule allows."

"Pete, I'd be delighted to talk with you about working with your company! Just give me a call when you know your schedule, and we'll find a time to chat. And oh, by the way, I have something for you." Kip handed Pete a small envelope. On the outside was the phone number in Los Angeles where he could be reached. A single sheet of paper was inside. Pete slipped the envelope into his coat pocket.

The train slowed and stopped. Kip and Pete left the compartment together, stepped out into the cool Los Angeles air, and followed the other passengers toward the terminal exit. A line of taxis were queued up near the curb. Just before ducking into his cab, Kip waved and called out to Pete, "Good luck with your meeting!"

Pete smiled and waved back, "Thanks, I'll let you know how it went when I call you."

Pete realized that he had a long road ahead of him. Kip had made that plain. After this meeting in L.A., he would be going back to headquarters to find people who wanted to start this new journey with him. Pete couldn't stop thinking about how the new CFO would react to these ideas and worried about whether the board would give him the time necessary to make the change.

As Pete's cab pulled away from the curb, he reached into his coat pocket and withdrew the paper from inside the envelope. On one side Kip had written 'Ten Control-Based Ideas That Destroy Accountability'; on the other side was 'Three Freedom-Based Ideas That Create Accountability.'

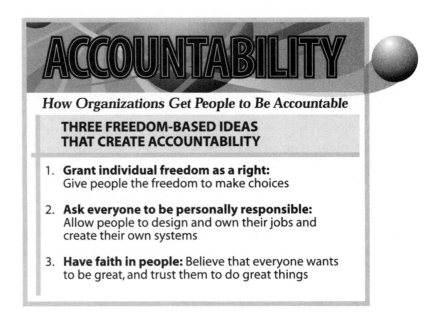

ACCOUNTABILITY

How Organizations Get People to Be Accountable

THREE FREEDOM-BASED IDEAS THAT CREATE ACCOUNTABILITY

1. **Grant individual freedom as a right:**
   Give people the freedom to make choices

2. **Ask everyone to be personally responsible:**
   Allow people to design and own their jobs and create their own systems

3. **Have faith in people:** Believe that everyone wants to be great, and trust them to do great things

ACCOUNTABILITY

How Organizations Get People to Be Accountable

TEN CONTROL-BASED IDEAS THAT DESTROY ACCOUNTABILITY

1. **Incentive programs and pay-for-performance plans:** Promote cheating and distract people from doing the "right thing" by encouraging the practice of "going for the dough no matter what!"

2. **Internal competition:** Destroys trust, discourages cooperation, and encourages hoarding of resources

3. **Performance reviews:** Devastate the human spirit by offering judgments rather than encouragement

4. **Forced ranking systems (another form of judgment):** Assume some people are unsalvageable, and give management an excuse not to deal directly with performance issues in a more proactive way

5. **Personal improvement plans (another form of judgment):** Send the message that people are "broken" and need to be "fixed"

6. **Managing people:** Makes the manager accountable, not the employee, and suggests people need watching

7. **Restrictive policies and procedures:** Inhibit creative solutions that lie outside established policies and procedures; and, by demanding compliance, give people an excuse not to be accountable for making wise choices

8. **Employee recognition programs:** Discount the contributions of those who are not recognized, encourage suck-ups, and foster office politics

9. **Missions, visions, and values statements:** Imposed from the top, are seen by most as mere wallpaper that, at best, are ignored; at worst, create cynicism

10. **Traditional job descriptions:** Restrict personal initiative by telling people what they don't do

THE FREEDOM SURVEY™ (FS™)

This brief survey lists seven organizational elements. For each element, check the statement that *most* closely describes your organization's approach to that element. The statement you check should reflect *how you experience your organization today,* not what others in the organization might think or how you would like your organization to be.

A scoring sheet immediately follows the survey. Your score indicates the level in which you believe your organization is operating. A brief description of each level is included to help you verify your score.

Check only one response under each of the seven organizational elements that most closely corresponds to the statement "*Most* like my organization."

1. WORK ENVIRONMENT—How *Controls* Are Used:

_____ A. Subtle forms of control are used to indirectly influence individual and group behaviors.

_____ B. Strict controls are put in place to ensure compliance with authority.

_____ C. Controls have been abandoned; people are expected to take personal responsibility for their choices.

_____ D. Incentives are used to control individual and group activity.

2. CHANGE STRATEGY—How *Organizational Change* Is Accomplished:

_____ A. Organizational change is initiated and driven from the top.

_____ B. Organizational change is accomplished by getting individuals to improve their attitudes.

_____ C. Organizational change is brought about by getting people to compete for limited resources and rewards.

_____ D. Organizational change is accomplished by promoting a willingness to experiment with new ideas.

3. MOTIVATIONAL PHILOSOPHY—How *People Perform Best:*

_____ A. People will perform best when they are trusted to do their best. Those who cannot be trusted are asked to leave.

_____ B. People will perform best when they are offered an incentive to do so.

_____ C. People will perform best when their work is regularly assessed.

_____ D. People will perform best if they follow directions precisely.

4. LEADERSHIP STYLE—How *Leaders Distribute Responsibilities:*

_____ A. Leaders in our organization delegate responsibilities to individuals and work groups as they see fit.

_____ B. Leaders in our organization allow people to take on additional responsibilities depending on how well they do on their personal evaluations and performance assessments.

_____ C. Leaders in our organization act primarily as a resource to individuals and groups who have taken complete responsibility for designing and performing their jobs.

_____ D. Leaders in our organization award responsibilities to those that perform best compared to their peers.

5. MANAGEMENT STRUCTURE—How *Accountability* Is Established:

_____ A. Accountability in our organization is ensured through adherence to rules, policies, and procedures.

_____ B. Accountability in our organization belongs to the people who choose the responsibilities they want and are accountable for the results.

_____ C. Accountability in our organization is verified through process measurement and job certification systems.

_____ D. Accountability in our organization is confirmed through the use of periodic personal evaluations and performance assessments.

6. CAREER ADVANCEMENT SYSTEM—How *Jobs* Are Distributed:

_____ A. In our organization, promotions are awarded to those who perform best compared to those competing for the same job.

_____ B. In our organization, those in authority design the job descriptions, make the work assignments, and promote individuals as they see fit.

_____ C. People in our organization are encouraged to try new things, to design their own jobs, and to develop their own career plan.

_____ D. People in our organization are promoted depending on how well they score on periodic performance reviews.

7. STAFFING STRATEGY—How *Staff Members* Are Recruited:

_____ A. We look for people who will respond positively to feedback from supervisors, and will show personal improvement in a timely manner.

_____ B. We look for people who will comply with those in authority and do what they are told.

_____ C. We look for people who will cooperate with the supervisors and compete well with their peers.

_____ D. We look for people who are capable of managing themselves, will ask for help when they need it, and can work well with others.

Scoring the Freedom Survey™

Circle the points for each of the seven questions corresponding to "*Most* like my organization," and then total your score.

	Most Like My Organization	Points
1. How Controls Are Used:	A	3
	B	1
	C	4
	D	2
2. How Organizational Change Is Accomplished:	A	1
	B	3
	C	2
	D	4
3. How People Perform Best:	A	4
	B	2
	C	3
	D	1
4. How Leaders Distribute Responsibilities:	A	1
	B	3
	C	4
	D	2
5. How Accountability Is Established:	A	1
	B	4
	C	2
	D	3
6. How Jobs Are Distributed:	A	2
	B	1
	C	4
	D	3
7. How Staff Members Are Expected to Behave:	A	3
	B	1
	C	2
	D	4

Total Points Circled _____

Interpreting Your Freedom Survey Score

Level 1: 7–10
Your organization uses the "Top-Down" approach. Controls and organizational change are imposed from the top. People are expected to do what they are told, with leaders delegating responsibilities as they see fit. Accountability is imposed through the use of strict rules, policies, and procedures. Those in authority assign jobs, and people are expected to do what they are told.

Level 2: 11–17
Your organization uses the "Incentive-Driven" approach. Incentives and internal competitions are used both to control the organization and to drive organizational change. People are expected to compete well, and leaders award additional responsibilities to top performers while taking away responsibilities from poor performers. Accountability is verified through the use of scoring and certification systems. The best jobs go to those who have performed best compared to their peers and cooperate with their supervisors.

Level 3: 18–24
Your organization uses the "Conditional Freedom" approach. Organizational change is brought about by getting individuals to focus on personal improvement. Periodic personal evaluations and performance appraisals are used to assess improvement, to distribute responsibilities, to assign jobs, and to establish accountability. Staff members are expected to respond positively to feedback from supervisors.

Level 4: 25–28
Congratulations—your organization uses the "Freedom-Based" approach. Individual freedom, personal responsibility, and a faith and trust in people have replaced all forms of control. People take responsibility for designing their jobs, for

choosing their projects, and for being accountable for the results. Those who cannot be trusted to take responsibility and be accountable either have already left the organization or soon will be asked to leave. Organizational change is accomplished by promoting a willingness to experiment with new ideas. People are expected to manage themselves, to work well with others, and to ask for help when they need it.

N O T E S

Chapter 3
1. Harley-Davidson USA, Annual Report, 2000.

Chapter 4
1. B. F. Skinner, *The Behavior of Organisms: An Experimental Analysis* (Englewood Cliffs, NJ: Prentice Hall, 1938; out of print).

Chapter 5
1. Edward L. Deci, *Why We Do What We Do: Understanding Self-Motivation* (New York: Penguin, 1995).
2. Alfie Kohn, *Punished by Rewards: The Trouble with Gold Stars, Incentive Plans, A's, Praise, and Other Bribes* (Boston: Houghton Mifflin, 1993).
3. John Kotter and James Heskett, *Corporate Culture and Performance* (New York: Free Press, 1992).
4. James Collins and Jerry Porras, *Built to Last: Successful Habits of Visionary Companies* (New York: HarperBusiness, 1997).
5. Allan Kennedy, *The End of Shareholder Value: Corporations at the Crossroads* (New York: Perseus, 2000).
6. Collins and Porras, *Built to Last.*
7. Ibid.
8. Richard deCharms, *Personal Causation: The Internal Affective Determinants of Behavior* (New York: Academic Press, 1968).

Chapter 6
1. Michael Beer, Russel A. Eisenstat, and Bert Spector, "Why Change Programs Don't Produce Change," *Harvard Business Review* (1998).
2. W. Edwards Deming, "The Fourteen Points," in *Out of the Crisis* (Cambridge, MA: Harvard University Press, 1986).

Chapter 7
1. Harold S. Kushner, *Living a Life That Matters: Resolving the Conflict between Conscience and Success* (New York: Knopf, 2001).
2. Thomas Lewis, Fari Amini, and Richard Lannon, *A General Theory of Love* (New York: Random House, 2000).

3. C. R. Cloninger, D. M. Svrakic, and T. R. Przybeck, "A Psychobiological Model of Temperament and Character," *Archives of General Psychiatry* (1993).

4. Paul Ekman, "Cross-Cultural Studies of Facial Expression," in *Darwin and Facial Expression: A Century of Research in Review* (New York: Academic Press, 1973).

5. Carol E. Izard, *The Face of Emotion* (New York: Appleton-Century-Crofts, 1971).

6. Lebow Research, *Values & Attitude Study (VAS)* (Bellevue, WA: Author, 2001).

7. Jerome Kagan, *Three Seductive Ideas* (Cambridge, MA: Harvard University Press, 1998).

8. Kushner, *Living a Life That Matters.*

9. Peter F. Drucker, "Beyond the Information Revolution," *Atlantic Monthly* (October 1999).

Chapter 8

1. Mort Meyerson, "Everything I Thought I Knew about Leadership Is Wrong," *Fast Company* (April 1996).

2. Ibid.

3. Elisabeth Kubler-Ross and David Kessler, *Life Lessons: Two Experts on Death and Dying Teach Us about the Mysteries of Life and Living* (New York: Scribner, 2000).

4. Katherine J. Sweetman, "Employee Loyalty around the Globe," *MIT Sloan Management Review* (Winter 2001).

Chapter 9

1. *Merriam-Webster's Collegiate Dictionary*, 10th ed. (Springfield, MA: Merriam-Webster, 1993).

2. Kathleen Norris, *Amazing Grace: A Vocabulary of Faith* (New York: Riverhead, 1998).

3. Robert Spector and Patrick D. McCarthy, *The Nordstrom Way* (New York: Wiley, 1995).

4. *Nordstrom Employee Handbook* (Seattle, WA: Nordstrom, n.d.).

5. Edward L. Deci, *Why We Do What We Do: Understanding Self-Motivation* (New York: Penguin, 1995).

6. Nathaniel Branden, *Taking Responsibility: Self-Reliance and the Accountable Life* (New York: Simon & Schuster, 1996).

7. Ibid.

8. Alfie Kohn, *Punished by Rewards: The Trouble with Gold Stars, Incentive Plans, A's, Praise, and Other Bribes* (Boston: Houghton Mifflin, 1993); Deci, *Why We Do What We Do.*

9. Deci, *Why We Do What We Do.*

10. Ibid.

Chapter 10

1. Lebow Research, *Shared Values Process®/Operating System (SVP/OS)* (Bellevue, WA: Author, 2002).

2. James A. Belasco and Ralph C. Stayer, *Flight of the Buffalo: Soaring to Excellence, Learning to Let Employees Lead* (New York: Warner, 1993).

3. James A. Autry and Stephen Mitchell, *Real Power: Business Lessons from the Tao Te Ching* (New York: Riverhead, 1998).
4. Rob Lebow and William L. Simon, *Lasting Change: The Shared Values Process That Makes Companies Great* (New York: Van Nostrand Reinhold, 1997).

Chapter 11
1. Malcolm Gladwell, *The Tipping Point: How Little Things Can Make a Big Difference* (New York: Little, Brown, 2000).
2. Ibid.
3. Lebow Research, *Values & Attitude Study (VAS)* (Bellevue, WA: Author, 2001).
4. Gladwell, *The Tipping Point.*

Chapter 12
1. Robert K. Greenleaf, *Servant Leadership: A Journey into the Nature of Legitimate Power and Greatness* (Mahwah, NJ: Paulist, 1983).
2. Lee G. Bolman and Terrence E. Deal, *Leading with Soul: An Uncommon Journey of Spirit* (San Francisco: Jossey-Bass, 1995).
3. Ibid.
4. James A. Autry and Stephen Mitchell, *Real Power: Business Lessons from the Tao Te Ching* (New York: Riverhead, 1998).
5. Jack Stack with Bo Burlingham, *The Great Game of Business* (New York: Doubleday, 1992).
6. Lebow Research, *Values & Attitude Study (VAS)* (Bellevue, WA: Author, 2001).

Chapter 14
1. Malcolm Gladwell, *The Tipping Point: How Little Things Can Make a Big Difference* (New York: Little, Brown, 2000).
2. Laurel Spitzer, Jeanne Kertes-Smith, and Tom Kertes, *The Readers Way: Understanding the Code* (self-published, 2001).
3. Gladwell, *The Tipping Point.*
4. Ibid.
5. Ibid.
6. Lebow Research, *Values & Attitude Study (VAS)* (Bellevue, WA: Author, 2001).

Chapter 15
1. Lebow Research, *Values & Attitude Study (VAS)* (Bellevue, WA: Author, 2001).
2. Jon R. Katzenbach and Jason A. Santamaria, "Firing Up the Front Line," *Harvard Business Review* (May–June 1999).

Chapter 16
1. Hal F. Rosenbluth and Diane McFerrin Peters, *The Customer Comes Second and Other Secrets of Exceptional Service* (New York: Morrow, 1992).

2. Ibid.
3. Egon Zehnder, "A Simpler Way to Pay," *Harvard Business Review* (April 2001).
4. Ibid.
5. Tom Coens and Mary Jenkins, *Abolishing Performance Appraisals: Why They Backfire and What to Do Instead* (San Francisco: Berrett-Koehler, 2000).
6. Max DePree, *Leadership Is an Art* (New York: Bantam Doubleday Dell, 1989).
7. Edward M. Hallowell, "The Human Moment at Work," *Harvard Business Review* (January–February 1999).
8. Richard Teerlink, "Harley's Leadership U-Turn," *Harvard Business Review* (July–August 2000).
9. Ibid.

Chapter 17

1. Lebow Research, *Values & Attitude Study (VAS)* (Bellevue, WA: Author, 2001).
2. Ibid.
3. Sasha Smith, "The Great Escape," *Forbes Small Business* (March 2001).

G L O S S A R Y

Accountability taking personal responsibility for one's own choices and for the results of those choices to oneself and to others.

Autonomy ability to govern oneself and to initiate one's own activity.

Behaviorism a theory of human behavior originally put forward by Harvard psychologist B. F. Skinner that posits individuals are conditioned through "operant conditioning" to respond to various stimuli.

Broken windows theory theory of criminal behavior offered by James Q. Wilson and George Kelling: "Crime is the inevitable result of disorder"; that is, broken windows left unrepaired lead to more broken windows which in turn create an invitation to criminals to commit more serious crimes.

Collectors people who love to share new ideas with others; they prospect for ideas in books, newspapers, magazines, the Internet, and even junk mail; they read more, listen more, and watch more than the average person.

Connectors people who have hundreds or thousands of "loose acquaintances" and who have a special gift for bringing people together.

Control-based philosophy a system of beliefs based on the idea that people cannot be trusted and must be held accountable by putting controls in place.

Corporate culture the social/psychological environment of an organization along with its systems of accountability.

Dissidents   people who find subtle ways to express their discontent through noncooperation or resistance; they are apt to complain openly to coworkers, may be disruptive during group meetings, and feel justified in withholding truth and trust.

Extrinsic motivation   the use of some external reinforcement, such as the offer of a reward or the threat of punishment, to encourage "correct" behavior.

Faith in people   rather than believing that people are incompetent, unmotivated, and irresponsible, faith in people says that people, regardless of race, creed, national origin, or gender, possess talent, internal motivation, and a desire to be great.

Fear-based environments   environments that depend on fear as the primary motivator of human behavior.

Financial steward   a person who protects the financial health and longevity of the organization.

Freedom-Based Philosophy™   a belief that people can be trusted and that freedom with responsibility is the best way to achieve accountability and sustainable results.

Freedom with responsibility   see *Freedom-Based Philosophy*.

Hero   a person who exhibits extraordinary selflessness in bringing people together, taking great delight in helping others succeed.

Incentives   inducements offered to get people to behave "correctly."

Inclusive communities   a place where all kinds of people can flourish and where they are free to develop their talents and interests.

Individual freedom   having the opportunity to be the author of one's own choices and to be accountable for the consequences of those choices.

Intrinsic motivation   doing an activity for the sheer "joy" of it; choosing an activity for the reward that is inherent in the activity itself.

Keen Internal Vision™   a shared vision of an organization's future that connects an individual's work to the larger purpose of the organization.

Law of the Few   one of Malcolm Gladwell's three laws of social epidemics: those special people who start social epidemics (mavens, connectors, and salesmen).

Maverick   a person who prefers to be independent; mavericks tend to gravitate to jobs where the bulk of their time may be spent working alone; they are often more interested in creatively pursuing ideas than in interacting with others.

Mentor   someone who freely shares knowledge, skills, and experience with others.

Nine-to-Fiver™   a person who works hard from nine to five and does his or her very best while at work but may be instinctively unwilling to take risk.

Operant conditioning   a theory that holds that an action may be controlled by a stimulus that comes after it rather than before it; that is, when a reward or "reinforcement" follows a behavior, that behavior is likely to be repeated.

Owning your job   taking responsibility for job responsibilities by asking four questions: (1) What responsibilities should I own? (2) What responsibilities should I not own? (3) What responsibilities should I share with others? (4) What new responsibilities should I take on?

Performance evaluation   a control-based method of evaluating employee performance; the stated purpose of most evaluation systems is to motivate employees to improve their performance by grading their past performance; however, when evaluated, most people feel judged and demotivated.

Personal responsibility   the idea that individuals should be able to own their jobs and own the organization's systems.

Persuader   a person who is particularly adept at convincing others to embrace new ideas; persuaders have the ability to convince even the toughest skeptics; through sheer enthusiasm, energy, and charm, they are able to win over doubters

Power of Context   one of Malcolm Gladwell's three laws of social epidemics: the social environment which allows a critical mass of people to become ignited with an idea.

Resource Provider™   one of the roles of a Wise Counsel™: to provide individuals and groups with the money, time, supplies, or expertise needed to complete tasks or projects.

Responsibility-Taking™ Keys   the eight responsibilities needed to get every Member-Citizen® to become accountable; they include planning, priority setting, removing roadblocks, creativity, task completion, risk taking, policy setting, and self-expression.

Shared Values Principles®   The eight principles identified by Lebow Research in 1988 from seventeen million surveys worldwide: Treat Others with Uncompromising Truth, Lavish Trust on Your Associates, Mentor Unselfishly, Be Receptive to New Ideas Regardless of Their Origin, Take Personal Risk for the Organization's Sake, Give Credit Where It Is Due, Do Not Touch Dishonest Dollars, and Put the Interests of Others before Your Own (reference the Shared Values Process®/Operating System).
Important note: These eight principles are directly linked to an operation's present and future success and can be used to predict future financial performance, merger challenges, employment candidates fitting into a particular department and equity investments—see *ValuesCHQ™*.

Shared Values Process®/Operating System   the People Operating System based on seventeen million people's answers to what would allow them to "play at the top of their game." Surveyed from forty countries around the world, the Process is registered and trademarked by the U.S. federal government by the Lebow Company since 1989 and is supported by a five-module, 1,500-page curriculum with fully supported facilitator notes.

Task force   a small group (usually eight to twelve individuals) assembled to study an operational issue and to formulate a recommended course of action.

Three Rules of Epidemics   Malcolm Gladwell's theory of "social epidemics"; they include the Power of Context, the Law of the Few, and the Stickiness Factor.

Values & Attitude Study™ (VAS)   a normalized and indexed study of Workplace Wellness™ addressing twenty-seven elements in a work environment in three groups: People Values®, Job Satisfaction, and People Systems® & Processes (reference Lebow Research—ValuesCHQ).

ValuesCHQ™ Workplace Wellness™ company that standardizes on a scale of 1 to 10 excellent places to work. Contact Lebow Company directly for more information.

Values Tension™ The tension gap that results when personal expectations for Shared Values behavior does not match the organization's ability to deliver Shared Values behavior.

Values Tension Index™ an organization's Values Tension® score indexed against the International Benchmark Average® score and the World Class Standard® score.

Visionary Leaders™ People who have a Keen Internal Vision®, are serious about ensuring the survival and success of the organization, and have great compassion for people.

Waiting to be asked™ a strategy employed by Wise Counsels® in order to allow individuals and groups to be responsible and accountable.

Wise Counsel™ an individual in a Quadrant Four organization (freedom-based workplace) who feels free to share information and knowledge with coworkers without the fear of losing power or influence.

I N D E X

Index

ACKNOWLEDGMENTS

"Dad, why don't you write a book?"
—Heather Spitzer, Randy's daughter

In January 2001, at a conference at the Haas Business School at Berkeley, California, I met Steven Piersanti, president of Berrett-Koehler Publishers, and briefly discussed a new book Randy Spitzer and I were working on. The working title was *Accountability*. Randy had begun the project more than one year earlier, and about five months prior to my conversation with Steven, I'd joined in collaboration. Steven's curiosity was peaked by the subject and our focus, and he asked me to send what we had. Frankly, I was reluctant to send Steven anything because the concepts were still half-baked, and I was afraid of the rejection. But I did as I promised and sent off the unfinished work with fingers crossed.

A few days later, Steven called, and we spent over an hour on the phone talking about the project. I was somewhat stunned and immediately called Randy with my good news. I assured Randy, a first-time author, that what was happening only happened in the movies—and that perhaps this was too good to be true, so we should keep this news to ourselves. What Steven said in the conversation I initially took with a grain of salt because Steven was talking about wanting to participate in the process. He spoke of a collaborative process between his staff and us. He talked like this approach was commonplace at Berrett-Koehler. Having been the author of two prior works in the past ten years, my experience with publishers is less than one of collaboration. I'd have to say it was more like a hit and run with the author left in the gutter bleeding.

Steven, it turned out, is not your run-of-the-mill publisher who pushes a new book off on subordinates. No, this publisher is different.

For most writers, Berrett-Koehler is a "pinch-me experience"—a publisher who care about more than the bottom line. Steven and his editorial staff collaborated with us. Their walk has been their talk throughout the project.

For this experience both Randy and I are deeply grateful. What began two years earlier as a research paper attempting to bring together hundreds of theories and writings around one central theme, accountability, with the help of Steven Piersanti and his staff, blossomed into a book that we are all proud of.

Additionally, we would like to thank all of those who helped us in the development of this book by courageously reading the early versions and digging into the subject with enthusiasm and constructive candor. Berrett-Koehler asked a group of wonderful people to read our early work. We thank Christine Saponara, Douglas Hammer, Richard Lynch, Christopher Delgado, Marcia Daszko, and Ariel Jolicoeur for their insights and ideas. A special thanks needs to go to Angela Wagner and Kathleen Epperson for their high level of creative thinking, contribution, and belief in the subject and in us. Jeevan Sivasubraminiam was great at getting to the point and helping us understand. His courage to ask tough questions and to challenge us on every page was invaluable. The Berrett-Koehler team practices accountability every day, for you don't write a book alone.

A special thanks goes to our wives, Sharon Lebow and Laurel Spitzer, for helping us add a human touch to our writing. Thanks to Jane Alberts, our editor, and to Pam Halvorson, my wonderful assistant who was with us every step of the way.

Finally, thanks to our book agent, Bill Gladstone, who has stuck by this project and was instrumental in getting this book into print. Bill is a one-in-a-million guy who has believed in me for nearly twenty years and whom I consider a friend.

—Rob Lebow

Rob Lebow is chairman of the Lebow Company and co-chairman of *Tomorrow's Workplace, Inc.* He is an internationally known keynote speaker, writer, and Wise Counsel™ on the subject of Shared Values and the Freedom-Based Workplace. The focus of his message emphasizes how implementing a Freedom-Based Operating System can dramatically change an operation's ability to serve customers, increase revenues, promote quality in every process, and improve the bottom line.

In 1990, Rob wrote *A Journey into the Heroic Environment,* which became a best-seller and is now published in five languages. In 1998, he coauthored *Lasting Change* with William Simon.

His talks have motivated managers and staff alike to want to build a workplace based on the principles of *Accountability.* Rob's approach is dynamic, and his message is clear: "Stop managing people and treat them like adults. Start dismantling systems and processes that inhibit personal responsibility. Only hire people you trust, then trust them. Create a workplace that encourages and demands accountability; and if you have dead wood in your operation, it's management's fault—do something about it!" Rob's message is strong language for control-based operations, but for those organizations that have come to realize that they need to change the basic framework of their focus enterprise-wide, his talk is timely, relevant, and therapeutic.

Randy Spitzer is Executive Vice President of *Tomorrow's Workplace, Inc.* He is a *cum laude* graduate of Pacific Lutheran University and has spent twenty-eight years as an educator. For the past sixteen years, he has been involved in corporate training with organizations such as Pepsi-Cola Bottlers, AT&T-TCI, Anheuser-Busch, and Saudi Aramco.

He began his career as a teacher in Washington state and has served as vice president of Washington Music Educators Association. After becoming a Certified Financial Planner™, Randy served as president of the Olympic Financial Planners Association and chairman of Century Financial Services of Washington. An active member of his local community, he has been president of the Kiwanis Club of East Bremerton and a board member of the Bremerton Chamber of Commerce. Classically trained in vocal performance and choral conducting, Randy continues to perform as a frequent guest soloist and conductor. He is also the author of numerous book reviews, articles, and training manuals. *Accountability* is his first book.

ABOUT THE COMPANY

Lebow Company began operation in 1985 as a research organization. Today, it ranks as the leading training and research company in the areas of Shared Values and Shared Values research. Over the past seventeen years, the benchmarking instrument developed by Lebow Research—The Values & Attitude Study™ (VAS™)—has compiled over two thousand organizational sites in its database. The VAS details, correlates, and predicts future performance for an operation by comparing the level of Shared Values an operation exhibits against international benchmarks and world-class scores. Twenty-seven independent indices isolate an operation's performance, which is then correlated to financial health.

From this rich body of research, Lebow Company developed in 1992 the Shared Values Process®/Operating System and received protection from the United States Patent Office. Presently, over two hundred operations from the United States, Asia, Europe, Africa, and the Middle East have utilized the People Operating System to improve their overall performance. Organizations such as Ford Motor Company Asia Pacific Operations, Philippines and India; Saudi Aramco; U.S. Food Service; Pepsico; Engen Oil of South Africa; Trane American Standard; and many other operations from around the world have enjoyed introducing the Freedom-Based philosophy of Shared Values to their organizations. Additionally, the Lebow Company has served as a Government Services Agency (GSA) contractor for the past eight years.

For more information on Lebow Research (the Values & Attitude Study forecasting tool) and the Lebow Company (the Freedom-Based Shared Values Process®/Operating System for your organization), please get in touch with us directly. If you're interested in becoming a "Freedom-Based Distributor" or a "Freedom-Based Associate," please contact us directly with

some background on your interests and experience. We're looking for representation worldwide.

Lebow Company, Inc.
11820 Northup Way, Suite 101
Bellevue, WA 98005
(425) 828-3509
(800) 423-9327
Fax: (425) 828-3552
E-mail: Lebowco@aol.com
www.Lebowco.com

(ValuesCHQ™ and Tomorrow's Workplace are subsidiaries of
the Lebow Company, Inc.)